Anguel Stefanov

Kant's Conceptions of Space and Time and Contemporary Science

MINKOWSKI
Institute Press

Anguel Stefanov
Institute for the Study of Societies and Knowledge
Bulgarian Academy of Sciences
13a Moskovska Street
1000 Sofia
Bulgaria

ISBN: 978-1-927763-42-1 (softcover)
ISBN: 978-1-927763-43-8 (ebook)

Minkowski Institute Press
Montreal, Quebec, Canada
http://minkowskiinstitute.org/mip/

For information on all Minkowski Institute Press publications visit our
website at http://minkowskiinstitute.org/mip/books/

CONTENTS

1 INTRODUCTION

Why would someone who is interested in contemporary scientific ideas about space and time want to read a book about Kant's conceptions of them? My answer is that Kant's philosophy was hugely influential not only into the nineteenth century, but as some authors contend, it has stimulated A. Einstein's project about the theory of relativity. I make an attempt to show that some of Kant's ideas provide for the first time a base for the explication of the dependence between physics (the kind of physical forces) and geometry, between the nature of space and the symmetries of material bodies. As a first chapter the *Introduction* presents the aims and the original claims of the book.

Key words: aims of the investigation, original claims

This book is about Kant's pre-critical and transcendental conceptions of space and time and their relations to contemporary science, namely physics, cosmology, and philosophy of time. I hope that it will attract the interest not only of readers who are working in the field of the theory or/and the history of Kant's pre-critical and transcendental philosophy, but also of readers, who exhibit an interest in history of science and/or in the relation of philosophical ideas with scientific hypotheses.

One of the aims this investigation is chasing is to illuminate Kant's merit for making initial theoretical steps towards the contemporary spatio-temporal picture of the world. This aim is being achieved by supplying argumentation for the following claim:

(C_1) In two of his pre-critical works Kant had a specific contribution for the enunciation of ideas, which have later proved to be of significance for the formation of contemporary physical and cosmological theories (Einstein's theory of relativity and multiverse theories), and for the interpretation of mirror (a)symmetry.

The content of chapter 2 in this book offers a defense of (C_1), though this claim may seem at first glance to be a bold, and no less a curious contention.

Immanuel Kant was undoubtedly a prominent philosopher who has contributed to the scientific knowledge of his days. Kant-Laplace theory of the genesis and formation of the solar system suffices to be mentioned in this respect. It is also known that his critical philosophy has exerted an influence on Albert Einstein in laying the conceptual base of the theory of relativity, and this influence was recently revealed by Stephen Palmquist (2010; 2011). My arguments for (C_1), however, are of a different kind and do not refer to some conceptual influence on A. Einstein; at least not to an influence which has been discovered and officially recorded, but which still might have happened. The ideas that I have in mind here belong to works that have been written by Kant during his pre-critical period.

Four other aims of this work consist in lending support to the following claims:

(C_2) Paradigmatic criticisms of Kant's transcendental conception of space and time stem out of misunderstandings, underpinned by philosophers and scientists who are visible figures in their respective cultural (and ideological) circles.

(C_3) Kant's transcendental philosophy does not set up a conceptual barrier in front of pro-empirical, or intuitive, and theoretical concepts of space and time.

(C_4) The conviction that the cosmology of the Big Bang supplies a solution to the first of Kant's antinomies does not hold water.

(C_5) Transcendental aesthetic can provide a base for explaining the possibility of paradoxes stemming out of the conceptualization of space and time as separate autonomous entities.

Chapters 3 – 6 are dedicated to the achievement of these aims, respectively.

Like claim (C_1), claim (C_5) argues for the role of Kant's philosophy – this time of transcendental aesthetic – as a base for explaining the appearance of some well-known paradoxes connected with space and time, when the latter are being traditionally conceptualized as separate autonomous entities. The much debated problem today why we have a perceptual experience of time as flowing, while according to contemporary physics (and the B-theory of time) it does not flow, is also considered in chapter 6.

Unlike (C_1) and (C_5), the argumentation for claims (C_2) and (C_4) in chapters 3 and 5 respectively, has the purpose to elucidate the irrelevance of popular criticisms of Kant's transcendental conception of space and time, launched by well-known philosophers and scientists. This argumentation chases also the aim of finding the right epistemological meaning and role of philosophical and scientific ideas about the nature of space and time. (C_2) precedes the next three claims, because in order for readers to keep an interest in the next chapters, they ought to be certain beforehand that Kant's transcendental conception of space and time does not stay in contradiction to contemporary scientific theories.

The aim of chapter 4 is to provide argumentation for the claim (C_3), or in other words, for the possibility of conceptualizations of space and time. Paragraph 4.1 has a direct reference to transcendental philosophy through the attempt at explaining the reason why Kant speaks of "concepts of space and time" as well, in case that they are originally introduced to play the cognitive role of pure sensuous intuitions. In paragraph 6.2 some more details are attracted for the answer to the question how the birth of intuitive concepts of space and time could be accounted for. Paragraph 4.2 considers the emergence of theoretical concepts of space and time. They are not directly related to transcendental philosophy *per se*, but arguing for their possibility shows that this philosophy does not set up a conceptual barrier in front of the theoretical constructs of space and time (of space-time) in contemporary science.

The defense of the above formulated chief claims (C_1) – (C_5) is often connected with reconstructions of Kant's reasoning, as well as of that of his critics, and with the argumentation of appropriate auxiliary claims.Such reconstructions are put forward in 2.1, 2.2, and 3.2.

References in the text are given in brackets containing name of the author(s) (if not directly pointed to in the neighboring context), year of edition, and page(s); for example: (Palmquist 2011, 100).Exceptions are the references to Kant's *Critique of Pure Reason* which also include the abbreviation *CPR*, and the standard A and B indications for the first and second editions, for example (Kant 1966, 27, *CPR*, A: 26, B: 42). (Kant 1966) refers to F. Max Müller's translation, and (Kant 1998) to Paul Guyer's and Allen W. Wood's translation of Kant's first *Critique*.

4

REFERENCES

Kant, Immanuel. 1966. *Critique of Pure Reason.* Translated by F. Max Müller. Garden City, New York: Anchor Books, Doubleday & Company, Inc.

Kant, Immanuel. 1998. *Critique of Pure Reason.* Translated by Paul Guyer and Allen W. Wood. Cambridge: Cambridge University Press.

Palmquist, Stephen. 2010. "The Kantian Grounding of Einstein's Worldview: (I) The Early Influence of Kant's System of Perspectives." *Polish Journal of Philosophy* Vol. 4, N 1: 45-64.

Palmquist, Stephen. 2011. "The Kantian Grounding of Einstein's Worldview: (II) Simultaneity, Synthetic Apriority and the Mystical." *Polish Journal of Philosophy* Vol. 5, N 1: 97-116.

2 KANT'S PRE-CRITICAL THEORIZING OF SPACE REVISITED

The main subject of this chapter is the defense of the claim that pre-critical Kant had a specific contribution for the enunciation of ideas, which have proved later to be of significance for the formation of contemporary physical and cosmological theories. In his first book *Thoughts on the True Estimation of Living Forces* Kant puts forward the idea that worlds different from our own could probably exist within spaces having different properties and dimensions, determined by the type of the acting forces among substances. An interpretation is also suggested about the reason for the breaking of mirror symmetry, which is connected with Kant's argument from 1768, developed in his last pre-critical work *"On the First Ground of the Distinction of Regions in Space"*.

Key words: pre-critical period, dimensionality of space, other worlds, incongruent counterparts, mirror asymmetry.

As is traditionally accepted, Kant's pre-critical creative period is referred to the years 1746-1770, although his proper pre-critical project (dedicated mainly to the reconciliation of metaphysics and natural science) has a shorter span, covering the period from 1754 to 1766.[1] And it is worth noticing that in his first work, the book *Thoughts on the True Estimation of Living Forces*, written in 1746/1747 (Kant 1929)[2], as well as in his last work belonging to the pre-critical period –

---

[1]See in this connection the investigation made by Martin Schönfeld (2000, 4). According to this author, Kant's pre-critical period encompasses the years 1746-1780. Obviously he annexes the years known as "the silent decade" (from 1770 to 1780) to Kant's pre-critical creative period, although it is traditionally accepted that this period comes to an end in 1770, the year in which Kant defended his *Dissertation*.

[2]"Kant wrote the *Thoughts on the True Estimation of Living Forces* in 1746,

his essay "On the First Ground of the Distinction of Regions in Space", written in 1768 (Kant 1991), Kant is engaged with basic problems of space, concerning its nature and dimensionality.

The main subject of this chapter is the defense of claim (C₁), stating that pre-critical Kant had a specific contribution for the enunciation of ideas, which have proved later to be of significance for the formation of contemporary physical and cosmological theories, and for the interpretation of mirror (a)symmetry (see the *Introduction*). In paragraph 2.1 Kant's hypothesis about the possible existence of worlds requiring extensions (spaces) with properties and dimensions different from the three-dimensional Euclidean space will be considered. This hypothesis is a revolutionary one for the history of theoretical knowledge, being put forward almost a whole century before Lobachevsky, Bolyai and Riemann suggested the non-contradictory character of non-Euclidean geometries. And even more, as it will be brought out, this hypothesis of Kant has not an abstract geometrical origin, since it clearly connects space dimensionality with fundamental features of physical reality, like the law of gravity. Or as some authors argue,

> It seems to us that not only was Kant conscious, already in 1747, that the road to the comprehension of the dimensionality of space should involve both Physics and Mathematics [...], but, most importantly, that he set the basis for modern discussions of this fascinating theme (Caruso and Xavier 1996, 6).

Needless to say, this assessment stays in harmony with claim (C₁).

In paragraph 2.2 Kant's idea about a specific relation – not of objects towards objects, but of objects towards absolute space – through which left and right directions are differentiated, will be analyzed. A reconstruction of the so called Kant's argument of 1768 is being made, as well as a suggestion for the interpretation of mirror asymmetry.

---

added a dedication and a preface in 1747, and had it published in 1749" (Schönfeld 2000, 4).

2.1 The Possibility of Extensions with Properties and Dimensions Different from the Three-Dimensional Euclidean Space

As it was emphasized, and curious as it may seem, Immanuel Kant put forward the hypothesis about the possible existence of extensions with properties and dimensions different from the common three-dimensional Euclidean space, already in 1746. It was really a bold hypothesis for its time, since no scientist or philosopher before had admitted the validity of some other geometry to a world, different from ours. But are there worlds, really different from ours?

From a metaphysical point of view, Kant admits *the possible existence of such other worlds*. In his first work, *Thoughts on the True Estimation of Living Forces*, he tried to produce an argument of his own within the framework of the discussion between Leibnitz and the Cartesians about the nature and the formal presentation of the then so called "living force" (*vis viva*, whose importance was supported by Leibnitz), different from the purely mechanical force (*vis mortua*, known today to be the momentum, or the impulse of a moving body). Being now obsolete, this discussion will not be a matter of interest here.

> Kant's philosophical debut was a false start. He later considered the *True Estimation of Living Forces* a thorough embarrassment, which, for all practical purposes, it was. Not only was Kant incapable of resolving the problem of force, but also unbeknownst to him, Jean Le Rond d'Alembert had already published a theory that effectively settled the debate three years before Kant turned his mind to it. In the *Traite de Dynamique* (1743), d'Alembert argued for a scientifically promising conception of force and an assessment of the relevant formulas that implied the correct mathematical resolution of the controversy (Schönfeld 2000, 18-19).

However, Kant made an important theoretical digression from the proper historical controversy about the living forces that has a heuristic value, and that makes Schönfeld's assessment, though undoubtedly *correct* with respect to the historical facts, to be too exacting, concerning Kant's "thorough embarrassment, which, for all practical purposes, it was". This digression, exploiting metaphysical arguments, is the above mentioned claim about the possible existence of worlds, different from ours, suggested in §8 of the *Living Forces*. And it is just this hypothetical existence of many other worlds, which requires also the existence of spaces different from the three-dimensional Euclidean space, at least with respect to their dimensionality. But the claim in §8 is being preceded by a substantial metaphysical argument, presented in §7, which defies reason with the thought that some things could really exist, while they could be found nowhere within the world. Only after the argumentation developed in these two paragraphs of the *Living Forces*, Kant dares to ask the crucial question about the ultimate grounds for the three-dimensionality of the space of the world we inhabit, and to put forward his bold hypothesis about the possible existence of extensions with different properties and dimensions. This is why I'll firstly offer a reconstruction of Kant's reasoning presented in §§ 7-8 (Kant 1929, 8-9).

Kant's consideration begins with an elucidation of the sense in which one can support the view that a separate entity could occupy no definite place in space, exploits an accepted definition for the concept of world, and puts forward the metaphysical hypothesis about other existing worlds, though he gives a comment to the definition of world in the end of §8.[3] Kant's reasoning is based on the primary notions of *substance* and *force*, and could be reconstructed in the following way:

1. Every substance can exert a force directed outside it towards other substances and producing some action over them.

2. Since every substance, thought as a self-dependent existing entity, contains in itself the source of all its definitions, it is not necessary for its existence that it is in a dynamic relation with any other thing in the world.

3. Without outgoing forces from substantial objects, directed to other such objects, there are no mutual relations, and thus no order among them.

---

[3]Mundus est rerum omnium contingentium simultanearum et successivarum inter se connexarun series (World is an order of all contingent things, both simultaneous and successive, connected among themselves). Kant's comment amounts to the criticism that metaphysicists speak of only one existing world, and thus neglect the possibility for other worlds, composed of interconnected entities, which exert no forces on components of **our** world.

4. But without an order among objects no places in space exist, and having also in mind the possibility presumed by (2), it becomes clear that some entities could really exist, and yet be placed nowhere in the whole world.

5. If, according to (4), entities exist that are not connected with anything whatsoever in the world, they would not be a part of it; and if they participate in mutual relations of theirs, then they would form a whole of their own, which would represent a specific world, different from ours.

6. So, the metaphysical hypothesis comes to the fore, that it is completely possible that God has created many worlds, though their actual existence may still be undecided.

It is visible from (3) and (4) in the reconstruction done so far, that during the period when the *Living Forces* has been written, Kant was more under the influence of Leibniz than of Newton, concerning the nature of space. Indeed, the relational nature of space is presupposed in (3) and (4), and is clearly stated in the beginning of §9:

> It is easily proved that there would be no space and no extension, if substances had no force whereby they can act outside themselves. For without a force of this kind there is no connection, without this connection no order, and without this order no space (Kant 1929, 10).

This notwithstanding, at that time Kant was also well aware of Newton's conception of absolute space and time, which he will later pay a preference to (see 2.2), as well as of the classical law of mutual gravitational attraction.

Let us turn back to items (5) and (6) from the reconstruction of Kant's reasoning. The first one shows how a world, different from ours, could be formed: namely because of the specific connections among entities, secured by a definite force through which they interact (but different from the corresponding force, through which material bodies are connected in our world). And (6) is the ontological claim about the possible existence of many worlds, whose entities exhibit specific relations of their own. But (6) would remain only a curious metaphysical suggestion without much physical content and significance, if Kant had not supplied an answer to the crucial question: "What the specific dynamic relations among substances within a world depend on?" The answer is straightforward: they depend on *the form of the law* that determines the way in which substances act upon each other. So, the reconstruction of Kant's reasoning in §10 goes further as follows:

7. The specific dynamic relations among substances within a world, and to this effect *the space* of this world, depend on the form of the law according to which the substances by means of their essential forces act upon each other.

8. *The threefold dimension of space* of the existing world is due to the law, according to which the forces by which substances act on each other are inversely proportional to the square of the distances between them.

9. But this law is arbitrary (might have another form), and instead of it God might have chosen some other law (e.g. a law according to which the acting force is inversely proportional to the cube of the distance).

10. Then from this other law "an extension with other properties and dimensions would have arisen"; and "if it is possible that there are extensions with other dimensions, it is also very probable that God has somewhere brought them into being" (Kant 1929, 12).

Claim (7) is of a general ontological character and has a key position within Kant's reasoning. Namely this original hypothesis places Kant into the history of science as the first thinker who put forward the idea that there is an internal connection between the geometry of space, from the one side, and the form of the law through which substances interact among each other as constituents of a world, from another side. Thus *he was the first to connect geometry with physics* – a step that was theoretically realized 170 years later in the form of a full-fledged theory by Albert Einstein in his general theory of relativity.[4]

Claim (8) is a concrete reformulation of (7), having in mind the established validity of Newton's law of mutual attraction among material bodies, stating that the acting force is inversely proportional to the square of the distances between them. Namely this form of the law is responsible for the three-dimensionality of space, while another

---

[4]Let me remind to this effect the quotation at the beginning of this chapter from Caruso and Xavier (1996, 6).

form of the same law would correspond to a space with different dimensions. Thus *Kant supplies an explanation why the space of our world is three-dimensional.*

The question of the *physical* relevance of spatial dimension seems to arise first in the early work of Immanuel Kant.[...]5 He realized that there was an intimate connection between the inverse square law of gravitation and the existence of precisely three spatial dimensions, although he regards the three spatial dimensions as a consequence of Newton's inverse square law rather than *vice versa* (Barrow and Tipler 1986, 260).

It is correct indeed that the mathematical form of the gravitational potential is due to the three-dimensionality of physical space, and not *vice versa*. And Kant would have certainly put it the right way, had he not been influenced by the relational view about the nature of space at the time of writing the *Living Forces*. But what is important here is the gist of Kant's theorizing. This is the crystallization of the idea that "*there is an intimate connection between the inverse square law of gravitation and the existence of precisely three spatial dimensions*", and the Königsberg thinker was the first to put forward this novel idea. It was elaborated later by William Paley, Paul Ehrenfest, and Hermann Weyl.

In the twentieth century a number of outstanding physicists have sought to accumulate evidence for the unique character of physics in three dimensions. Ehrenfest's famous article[...] of 1917 was entitled '*In what way does it become manifest in the fundamental laws of physics that space has three dimensions?*' and it explained how the existence of stable planetary orbits, the stability of atoms and molecules, the unique properties of wave operators and axial vector quantities are all essential manifestations of space. Soon afterwards, Hermann Weyl [...] pointed out that only in (3+1) dimensional space-times can Maxwell's theory be founded upon an invariant, integral form of the action; only in (3+1) dimensions it is conformally invariant (Barrow and Tipler 1986, 260-261).

---

5 J. D. Barrow and F. J. Tipler have here in mind Kant's work *Thoughts on the True Estimation of Living Forces.*

12

Thus Kant's prophecy, stated by claims (7-8) from the reconstruction of his reasoning in the *Living Forces*, that there is an intimate relation between the characteristics of physical space and the form of the basic laws through which substances interact, has turned to be a guiding idea re-discovered by twentieth century theoretical physics. In a broader theoretical context, the idea is embedded into the Einstein's complex equation of general relativity. The one side of this equation represents the geometry of space-time, while the other side – the way of constitution and distribution of matter (including energy). In a word, *this is the idea of the interdependence between geometry and physics.*

If I am allowed a brief digression here concerning Einstein's theory of relativity, and quitting Kant's first pre-critical work, I can point to the interesting paper of Stephen Palmquist, in which he successfully argues that "Einstein's worldview had an essentially Kantian grounding":

> By relating my argument primarily to Einstein's *worldview* (i.e., to the set of background assumptions that guide one's thinking on almost everything), I am not claiming that Kant had a direct influence on the development of Einstein's specific *scientific* discoveries... What we have established up to now is only that certain key features of Kant's worldview seem to have informed Einstein's background assumptions (Palmquist 2010, 53).

The quotation is not only interesting by itself, since it throws some additional light on the central claim (C_1) of this chapter. (This is the claim that Kant had a specific contribution for the enunciation of ideas, which have later proved to be of significance for the formation of Einstein's theory of relativity and multiverse theories, and for the interpretation of mirror (a)symmetry.)I afford this brief digression tempted also by Palmquist's thesis about Kant's (and Einstein's) construal of the cognitive status of geometry that conforms to the main claims from the next chapter. According to this author, Kant makes a difference between the necessary and universal character of geometry, emerging from the subjective constitution of our perceptual capacity, and the actual but imperceptible geometry underlying the empirical world.[6] A pretension to represent the latter geometry, I can add, is

---

[6] As he writes: "Kant argues that Euclidean geometry's necessary and universal character derives not from any empirical connection between objects but from the subjective constitution of our perceptual capacity. This is compatible with

the spatio-temporal geometrical model of the theory of general relativity. It exploits the "imperceptible" four-dimensional Riemannian geometry.

Let us turn back to Kant's *Living Forces*. As we have already seen, Kant binds his reasoning with another bold hypothesis that has become a conceptual precursor of contemporary cosmological thinking, and thus also stays in support of (C_1). *This is the hypothesis about the probable existence of many worlds.* Leaving the famous many-worlds-interpretation of quantum mechanics aside, cosmologists speak often today about the possibility our visible universe to be only a small part from a bigger formation, usually called *multiverse*, encompassing many other universes like ours, or different from it. String theorists, as well as some proponents of the Big bang initiation of our universe, are convinced of the high probability of the multiverse hypothesis. But it was Kant's speculative thinking to raise for the first time the hypothesis about the possible existence of many words, each invisible from the point of view of the rest (see (5-6) above), since the substances inhabiting them submit to different kinds of dynamic interactions and conform to different spaces.[7] And it is worth noticing that the multiverse hypothesis goes out today from its speculative phase and enters an observational phase, secured recently by the detailed cosmic microwave background picture of the universe.[8]

In the end, I would like to point to *another conceptual insight of Kant concerning the birth of geometry as an abstract discipline* in §10 of the *Living Forces*. After his contention that another law of interaction among substances would lead to an extension with other properties and dimensions, Kant declares that

---

Einstein's view of geometry: both distinguish between the *geometry that can be described* (or pictured)–in its purest form, Euclidean geometry–and the actual (yet ultimately imperceptible) geometry underlying the empirical world." (Palmquist 2010, 51)

[7] Other thinkers before Kant have spoken of many worlds, but within our universe, while he was the first, as far as I know, to construe the worlds as cosmologically separated, because of the different spaces they fill up.

[8] On the 21st of March 2013 the European Space Agency announced that its Planck space telescope provided the most detailed map ever created of the cosmic microwave background – the relic radiation from the Big Bang. The map reveals the existence of features that challenge the foundations of our current understanding of the Universe. (http://www.esa.int/Our_Activities/Space_Science/Planck/Planck_reveals_an_almost_perfect_Universe). A temperature fluctuation within the map is being interpreted as an evidence for a gravitational influence of another universe upon ours.

> A science of all these possible kinds of space would un-
> doubtedly be the highest enterprise which a finite under-
> standing could undertake in the field of geometry (Kant
> 1929, 12).

So, in the end of the 40-ies of the 18th century Kant had the insight
of the birth of pure geometry as a science, almost a century before
non-Euclidean geometries to be put forward as consistent abstract
geometrical constructions.

2.2 Parity (A)Symmetry and Space

The central claim of this chapter (C_1) requires also some argument
to be provided for the contention that Kant's last pre-critical work of
1768 entitled "On the First Ground of the Distinction of Regions in
Space" (Kant 1991)[9] contains a consistent explanation for the presence
of incongruent counterparts being mirror image objects of each other. I
shall try to clarify that in this essay of Kant there is a hidden argument
for the possibility that mirror symmetry, called also parity symmetry
(mainly within the context of contemporary quantum theories), may
not be universally valid.

In a nutshell, Kant's claim in this essay is that if incongruent counterparts (as for instance left and right human hands) do really exist,
then absolute space must also exist. This is usually known as the
Kant's argument of 1768. Besides this work, Kant recalled about
incongruent counterparts in some later works belonging to his critical
period,[10] but altering the argument of 1768, in order to comply with
his turn to transcendental philosophy. Anyhow, as Van Cleve and R.
E. Frederick put it

> Kant's arguments, whatever the final verdict on them,
> are highly ingenious, and evaluation of them leads one into
> a number of fascinating topics. These include the possibil-
> ity of "higher" dimensions of space and the physicist's prin-
> ciple, now known to have exceptions, of parity, or right–left

---

[9]Original title: *"Von dem ersten Grunde des Unterschiedes der Gegenden im
Raume"*. Akademie edition of Kant's works: Kant AA II: Vorkritische Schriften
II, 1757-1777, S. 373-384.

[10]In his Inaugural Dissertation of 1770, in the *Prolegomena to Any Future Metaphysics* of 1783, and in the *Metaphysical Foundations of Natural Science* of 1786.

indifference of the laws of nature (Van Cleve and Frederick 1991, vii).

There is no verbal exaggeration, I assume, in the otherwise standard for the purpose of a "Preface" declaration that evaluation of Kant's arguments "leads one into a number of fascinating topics". Indeed, incongruent counterparts have something to do with the nature of space; but they are also exemplifications of mirror symmetry; and the latter leads us, through the prism of theoretical and experimental results of 20th century physics, to one key topic for contemporary science – the laws of conservation. These fundamental laws have not only a theoretical, but an enormous practical significance for humankind. In a world without laws of conservation of basic physical quantities (as are energy, momentum, angular momentum, electric charge, and the like), life would be certainly impossible. Different conservation laws, however, are dependent on different types of symmetry. So, if natural symmetries were broken (at least to some extent), then the corresponding laws of conservation would also have their limitations. Aesthetical considerations aside, this fact clearly shows why symmetries are so valuable. But mirror symmetry, although valid almost everywhere, is broken for some processes of decay of elementary particles. It follows then that the natural world is not perfectly symmetrical.

Kant certainly had no information about all this. But do scientists know today the reason why the natural world is not completely symmetrical?

Why is nature so nearly symmetrical? No one has any idea why. The only thing we might suggest is something like this: There is a gate in Japan, a gate in Nikko, which is sometimes called by the Japanese the most beautiful gate in all Japan; it was built in a time when there was great influence from Chinese art. The gate is very elaborate, with lots of gables and beautiful carvings and lots of columns and dragon heads and princes carved into the pillars, and so on. But when one looks closely he sees that in the elaborate and complex design along one of the pillars, one of the small design elements is carved upside down; otherwise the thing is completely symmetrical. If one asks why this is, the story is that it was carved upside down so that the gods will not be jealous of the perfection of man. So they purposely put the error in there, so that the gods would not be jealous and get angry with human beings.

We might like to turn the idea around and think that the true explanation of the near symmetry of nature is this: that God made the laws only nearly symmetrical so that we should not be jealous of His perfection! (Feynman et al. 1964, Ch. 52, 52-12).

Having in mind this revelation of the famous noble prize winner Richard Feynman, one should not wonder why philosophers today display different attitude towards Kant's pre-critical treatise "On the First Ground of the Distinction of Regions in Space" (hereafter *"On the First Ground"*). All the more that Kant has tried to go beyond the works of such great men of his time, as "the celebrated Leibniz" and the no less "celebrated Euler", as he respectfully calls them,[11] in seeking an explanation for the possibility of incongruent counterparts, and respectfully for mirror symmetry in nature. Nowadays there are authors who criticize Kant's argument of 1768, and his interpretation of incongruent counterparts in his *Dissertation* of 1770, attracting some new mathematical knowledge.

In recent times, a number of authors have systematically criticized Kant's 1768 'proof' of the reality of absolute space. Peter Remnant may have been the first do to so, but many others have since joined him... In fact, Kant himself abandoned his main conclusion soon after publication, favouring instead the doctrine of transcendental idealism. I do not see how the 1768 proof can be saved, nor will I defend it here.[...] However, in dismissing it some critics seem to have gone too far, and either failed to fully acknowledge Kant's contribution, or attributed to him thoughts he is unlikely to have had. Kant's treatment of incongruent counterparts in his *Dissertation* of 1770 has also met strong opposition. In particular, his claim that the difference between a pair of incongruent counterparts cannot be apprehended by means of concepts alone[...]has been taken to be a mathematical falsehood. Indeed, incongruent counterparts have been shown to be mathematically distinguishable, with no intuitions needed for that purpose (Severo 2005, 30).[12]

---

[11]See the very beginning of (Kant 1991, 27), as well as (Kant 1991, 28).

[12]As we shall see further in this paragraph, Kant's "1768 proof" is neither for-

I shall occasionally consider the relevance of such criticisms in the course of the analysis of *the reconstruction of Kant's argument of 1768* in his *"On the First Ground"*. The reconstruction is as follows:

(1) "When a body is perfectly equal and similar to another, and yet cannot be included within the same boundaries, I entitle it the incongruent counterpart of that other" (Kant 1991, 31). Incongruent counterparts are mirror image objects of each other. Left and right hands are incongruent counterparts.

(2) So, there is a difference in shape between incongruent counterparts, in spite of their similarity: a left glove cannot fit a right hand, and vice versa.

(3) This is an *inner difference* between incongruent mirror image objects, because it cannot be explained neither by the way of the spatial arrangement of their parts in relation to one another, nor by the spatial relations they bear to other objects. A hand would be either left or right, even if it was the only material object in the universe.

(4) The difference between incongruent counterparts could be explained solely on account of their relation to the regions in space towards which their respective ordering of the parts is directed, while regions "involve reference to the universal [or absolute] space as a unity of which every extension must be regarded as a part" (Kant 1991, 27).

(5) Then the difference between incongruent counterparts could be explained solely on account of their relation to absolute space.

(6) Hence, if incongruent counterparts like left and right hands do really exist, then absolute space exists and has a reality of its own.

Let me say a few words about the notion of incongruent counterparts. Left and right human hands are the favorite example of Kant for incongruent counterparts, since they really are, according to the definition in (1), "perfectly equal and similar to one another". They

---

mally dismissed, nor it is in need to be "saved", since it is not a part of contemporary scientific knowledge. But it has to be kept in mind as a regulative idea for the explanation of parity asymmetry. Otherwise I completely agree with Rogério P. Severo that "in dismissing it some critics seem to have gone too far...".

18

have the same size, and are similar concerning the structure of their
component parts – the fingers and the palm in their mutual arrangement. And yet, a left glove cannot cover a right hand, and vice versa,
which means, as Kant brings out, that they "cannot be included within
the same boundaries", and so they are a good example of incongruent counterparts. Kant refers also to other examples of this sort, as
screws, snail shells and scalene spherical triangles. All of them present
an object together with its mirror image.

Let us consider examples of geometrical objects on the plane of
this sheet of paper. In Figure 2.1 the two of them are mirror images
of each other.

$$\vdash \quad \dashv$$

Fig. 2.1

If the left one is rotated at 180 degrees around the touching point of
the two perpendicular segments, and then shifted to the right, it could
perfectly match with the right one. Then these geometrical objects are
said to be *congruent* counterparts. Following an established tradition,
I shall dub every motion of a geometrical object on the plane that includes rotations and translations *without quitting the two-dimensional
space of the plane*, a *rigid motion* (Frederick 1991, 3). Thus we can
say that every pair of two-dimensional mirror-image objects, such that
one of them can be superimposed on the other by rigid motion alone,
represents congruent counterparts.

However, there are geometrical objects on the plane, and some of
them very simple, which are not congruent in this sense, although
they are also mirror images of each other. Such a case is presented by
Figure 2.2.

$$\lrcorner \quad \llcorner$$

Fig. 2.2

The two geometrical objects are quite similar with respect to their
size and composition: the respective lengths of the longer and the
shorter shafts in each of the figures are equal, and the angle between
them is one and the same right angle. Yet the left figure cannot be
superimposed on the right one by rigid motion alone. However, the
figures *can match with each other*, if a rotation is done at 180 degrees

along the longer shaft of the left figure that will take its shorter shaft *out of the plane* and place it on it again, and then a movement to the right is done until the two figures match with each other. Though quite similar, these two mirror-image objects are *incongruent* counterparts, since the coincidence of their shape is not achievable by rigid motion in the plane, i.e. in the space of their own, but a space with an *additional dimension* is needed for this purpose, in our case a three-dimensional space. Within the two-dimensional space of the plane, where they are situated, they do not possess the same form. Generally speaking, incongruent counterparts within a space of n dimensions can be superimposed by the help of some appropriate rigid motion within $(n+1)$-dimensional space. A motion of this type may be called *dimensional* motion, following again Frederick's naming (1991, 5).

Kant's example with the left and right human hands is also an example of incongruent counterparts, but a more complex example, because the hands are three-dimensional objects. They cannot co-incide with one another by rigid motion in three-dimensional space, despite their similarity in structure and size as mirror-image objects. According to claim (2), left and right hands don't share the same form in three-dimensional space, since they "cannot be included within the same boundaries". But by the help of a dimensional motion in an imaginary space with *four* dimensions a left hand can be made to superimpose on the right one, and vice versa.

There is also another type of motion through which incongruent counterparts could be made to match each other. The space, however, which the incongruent counterparts inhabit, must be very special; it must be twisted and closed in itself. Using a pair of scissors, for instance, we can cut out a strip of paper with both geometrical objects from Figure 2.2 on it.

> We then twist the strip of paper once and join the ends with glue. What we have constructed is a Möbius strip. Now, without lifting [the left object] or changing any relations of distance and angle between its parts, we move it once around the strip. We can call this type of motion a *Möbius* motion. Spaces in which Möbius motion is possible are usually called non-orientable spaces. If Möbius motions are not possible, then the space is orientable. Oddly enough, after a Möbius motion [the two objects] can be made exactly congruent (Frederick 1991, 5).

Let us turn back to the reconstruction of Kant's argument of 1768. The first claim of it is mainly an introductory definition, but claim (2) states that *incongruent counterparts are different in shape*. This statement has been turned into a matter of controversy. Indeed, we have just seen how the two-dimensional geometrical objects from Figure 2.2 can be exactly superimposed either by the help of a rotation in three-dimensional space, or by a Möbius motion within the two-dimensional non-orientable space of the Möbius strip. Their achieved coincidence then suffices the sameness of their shape to be avowed as an observable fact. The same could be said about the left and the right hand. They also demonstrate sameness of shape, provided one of them undergoes a rotation within a four-dimensional space, or a Möbius motion in a three-dimensional non-orientable space, until a spatial coincidence between them is reached. Martin Gardner seems to stick to (the first part of) this argument (1991, 67-68), and Ludwig Wittgenstein clearly supports it:

> The right hand and the left hand are in fact completely congruent. It is quite irrelevant that they cannot be made to coincide.

> A right-hand glove could be put on the left hand, if it could be turned round in four-dimensional space (Wittgenstein 1961, 143 (6.36111)).

We are somehow tempted to say that the objects from Figure 2.2 have the same shape, since an appropriate rotation in the three-dimensional space can make them "completely congruent". They are certainly incongruent within the limits of the two-dimensional orientable plane of the sheet of paper, which they inhabit. But the three-dimensional space exists with no less certainty, and a rotation in this space around the longer shaft of the left object can lead to the congruence in question. But is a similar procedure concerning left and right hands a legal generalization, so that one can say, together with Wittgenstein, that the left and the right hands are "completely congruent" as well? Or in other words, do rotations in an imaginary four-dimensional space are really possible, like rotations in the three-dimensional space that we as living creatures inhabit? Peter Remnant, in spite of his critical attitude to Kant's argument of 1768, still declares that "I have no idea at all what it means to speak of rotating a fully qualified three-dimensional object through the fourth dimension"

(Remnant 1991, 56). I may add to his frank astonishment the remark that for all we know, a *physical* space with *four* standard *spatial* dimensions does not really exist (at least in our world).[13] And "I have no idea at all" whether a non-orientable three-dimensional manifold does really exist. But if such spaces have no real existence, rigid motions within them are also not real, being hardly imaginable at the same time. Thus it remains unclear how a left (right) hand could really be made congruent with a right (left) hand. One can insist to this effect that left and right hands are incongruent counterparts, and because of this, they are different in shape.

But what then about the geometrical objects presented in Figure 2.2? We have seen that their congruence is achievable through a rotation in three-dimensional space, the existence of which raises no doubt. But these objects belong to the two-dimensional plane, and do not inhabit the three-dimensional space. Is it arguable then to qualify left and right hands as incongruent counterparts, as they are, while admitting the congruence of the objects from Figure 2.2? The answer seems to tend to the negative. These geometrical objects are certainly incongruent counterparts within the proper space of their own. So we may conclude that incongruent counterparts, though very similar, *are different in shape*. This conclusion directly supports claim (2) from the reconstruction of Kant's argument of 1768.

Let us proceed now to the estimation of claim (3). It states that the difference in shape between incongruent mirror-image objects is an *inner difference*, because it cannot be explained neither by the way of the spatial arrangement of their parts in relation to one another, nor by the spatial relations they bear to other objects. This claim from the reconstruction of Kant's argument of 1768 is a central one, since it paves, through the transitory claim (4),[14] the way to the concluding

---

[13]String theorists and some contemporary cosmologists work with an eleven-dimensional space. However, the additional spatial dimensions to the three common dimensions of the ordinary three-dimensional physical space are compactified as tiny tubes, so that classical rotations of physical bodies through them (and through which of them?) are impossible.

[14]Claim (4) is an expression of Kant's conviction that space is one-and-universal – a thesis that is transferred to his transcendental aesthetic with an essential change in the meaning of "universal", since the last predicate no more refers to an absolute Newtonian space. In "*On the First Ground*" Kant maintains that "absolute space is not an object of an outer sensation, but a fundamental concept which first makes all such sensations possible" (Kant 1991, 32). In his later critical works, pointed out in fn. 10 (but without his first *Critique*), Kant transforms his argument of 1768 into the claim that the difference between incongruent counterparts "cannot be apprehended except by pure intuition" (Kant 1929a, 60), i.e. incongruence

claims (5) and (6). It is not strange then that exactly claim (3) bears the main burden of the extant criticisms. The fact that the difference in shape between a left and a right hand cannot be explained by the way of the spatial arrangement of their parts in relation to one another seems arguable. But claim (3) states also that we are confronted with an "inner" difference between these incongruent counterparts, because *a hand would be either left or right, even if it was the only material object in the universe.* In Kant's words:

> If we conceive the first created thing to be a human hand, it is necessary either a right or a left, and to produce the one a different act of the creating cause is required from that whereby its counterpart can come into being (Kant 1991, 32).

Different critics of Kant try to reject just this last statement, or at least to cast some doubt on it. Some of them try to bring out the conventional status of terms like "left" and "right" (Gardner 1991, 64-65), but this fact begs the question with the stated inner difference between incongruent counterparts. Other critics bring out that a solitary human hand can neither be left or right, since an asymmetric reference object is needed for such estimation.[15] But if the left or right handedness of a hand does not exist *per se*, without a reference object to be found in space alongside the hand, then claim (3) loses its argumentative force. And even worse, the relational nature of space peeps behind the alleged refutation of (3), because the concrete (left or right) handedness ceases to be a matter of relation between a lone hand and absolute space.

The argument against (3) runs as follows. Let us imagine, as Kant suggests, that the first created thing in the world is a human hand. We could not say in this case whether it is left or right. We may be sure that one of these qualifications is correct only if another object comes into being, and which is suitable enough, so that this qualification is a result of the relation of the hand to the referent object. Let the

---

cannot be explained conceptually. This claim of Kant's has become a subject of criticism, in so far as some authors contend that incongruence is susceptible to representation by mathematical concepts (Mühlhölzer 1992), while in a recent paper Sven Bernecker "develops a new interpretation of Kant's argument from incongruent counterparts to the effect that the representations of space and time are intuitions rather than concepts" (2010, 519).

[15] See in this connection the views called "Externalism" and "Internalism" by James Van Cleve (1991, 206-210).

latter be a handless human body, created after the hand came into existence. Then we may see to which of the two wrists of the body the hand would match. Suppose it matches the right wrist. Thus the right-handedness of the hand would be ascertained. But without the referent body *no right-handedness of the lone hand exists*. Its right-handedness appears as a relation to the handless body and is not a property of the hand as such, if it were the only existing thing in the universe.

There is a strong *objection to this criticism*. Let us revisit Kant's story with the solitary hand. It was the only thing that existed in the universe, till the handless human body came into existence. The counter-argument states that the hand *was* a right one even before the body was created. Indeed, the creation of the handless body does not affect the nature of the hand that had been created before the body. Its creation does not affect the spatial characteristics of the region where the hand was situated, as well. But if so, then it certainly follows that the solitary hand had been right all the time of its existence, and the referent body only serves for its right-handedness *to be observed, and in no way to be created*. Thus Kant is right to contend that the difference between incongruent counterparts could be explained solely on account of their relation to absolute space, which is the proper content of claim (5). Claim (6) is a trivial consequence of claims (4) and (5), and as it seems it is supported by Kant as an explicit refutation of the relational conception of space, defended by Leibniz.

It may seem that the argumentation in favour of the reconstruction of Kant's argument of 1768 has come to an end. Notwithstanding its cogency, however, a "dark place" in the argumentation still exists. It is to be found in the lack of a more detailed interpretation of claim (5). Let me say it again: I do not call in question the transition from claim (3) to claims (4) and (5), but I note only the lack of a lucid meaning of Kant's contention that an incongruent counterpart stands in a relation to absolute space. This "dark place", as I called it, is presented by P. Remnant (1991, 55) as follows:

> It is not at all clear what properties space is supposed to possess in order that right hands and left hands should stand in different relations to it; presumably some sort of pervasive asymmetry. However I shall leave these questions aside...

"However", P. Remnant raised an essential question that I am not going to "leave it aside". And not only because it is essential, but also because it is closely connected with the "hidden argument" mentioned at the beginning of this paragraph, an argument for the hypothesis that mirror symmetry could eventually be broken somewhere in the world, although this fact caused the astonishment of the scientists two centuries after the publication of *"On the First Ground"*. Making the hidden argument explicit would finish the argumentation of the central claim of this chapter (C_1), according to which in his last pre-critical work Kant suggests an explanation of this unexpected fact. How this hidden argument could be made explicit?

If claims (3), (4), and (5) are taken to be correct, i.e. if incongruent mirror objects display an inner difference, which could be explained solely on account of their relations to absolute space, then the relation of the one incongruent counterpart to absolute space must be *different* from the corresponding relation of the other incongruent counterpart. Kant has certainly this fact in mind when insisting in the adduced quotation above that if instead a solitary right (left) hand a left (right) one had to be created *"a different act of the creating cause is required from that whereby its counterpart can come into being"*. A different act of the creating cause, however, would produce another result, which means that it is not excluded on principal grounds that incongruent counterparts could bear different observable properties, outside the fact of their geometrical similarity. Kant himself points to some examples to illustrate this possibility.

> Since the different feeling of right and left side is of such necessity to the judgment of regions, Nature has directly connected it with the mechanical arrangement of the human body, whereby one side, the right, has an indubitable advantage in dexterity and perhaps also in strength... But if some investigators, e.g. Borelli and Bonnet, are to be believed, while the right hand seems to have the advantage over the left in mobility, the left has the advantage over the right in sensibility. Borelli likewise assigns to the left eye, and Bonnet to the left ear, the possession of a greater sensibility than the corresponding organ on the right side (Kant 1991, 30).

Because of the different relations of incongruent counterparts to absolute space, the hypothesis is also not excluded on principal grounds that *another kind of mirror asymmetry could be observed, as well*: a difference not only in properties exhibited by right and left hands, as described by Kant above, but a mirror (parity) asymmetry concerning the frequency of appearance of the one incongruent counterpart over the other. This would be possible, provided that, as P. Remnant has put it, absolute space "presumably has to possess some sort of pervasive asymmetry". This asymmetry would be expected then to have a reflection over the material structure of incongruent mirror objects, at least in some cases. This is a hypothesis which Kant himself has assumed by his statement that:

> my aim in this treatise is to investigate whether there is not to be found in the intuitive judgments of extension, such as are contained in geometry, an evident proof *that absolute space has a reality of its own, independent of the existence of matter, and indeed as the first ground of the possibility of the compositeness of matter.*[16]

That absolute space, as a reality of its own, can be looked upon "*as the first ground of the possibility of the compositeness of matter*" is an original idea, put forward by Kant, and having an explanatory potential regarding parity (a)symmetry. This idea was not further elaborated in his *"On the First Ground"*,[17] but yet it was the Königsberg thinker who raised it 150 years before A. Einstein related through his famous complex equation space-time geometry with the "compositeness of matter", and almost two centuries before Tsung-Dao Lee of Columbia University and Chen-Ning Yang of Brookhaven National Laboratory reported in 1956 about experiments showing parity asymmetry in the weak interaction of β-decay of the nuclei of the element cobalt-60. Scientists then were really astonished by the fact of parity violation, but probably pre-critical Kant of 1768 would not be surprised, if he would have heard of this result.

The latter opinion may seem to be a wishful exaggeration. But let me make use of J. Earman's example, and look at the weak interaction in which a negative pi meson (π^-) and a proton (p) decay into a neutral hyperon (Λ^0) and neutral K meson (K^0), and then a subsequent decay occurs of the hyperon into another negative pi meson and a proton

---

[16](Kant 1991, 28), *original italics*.

[17]Kant could hardly elaborate further this idea, having in mind his conviction that the inner difference between incongruent counterparts is not presented conceptually, because "whatsoever in the outline of a body exclusively concerns its reference to pure space, can be apprehended only through comparison with other bodies", i.e. in intuition (Kant 1991, 32).

26

(Earman 1991, 246). The momentum vectors of the particles in the initial decay process lie in a plane, but the momentum vector of the negative pi meson (π^-) in the subsequent decay of the Λ^0 particle is at an angle to this plane. If mirror symmetry were not violated, then the process in which the momentum vector of the π^- particle is mirror symmetrically directed would be expected with the same frequency. But the experiment does not confirm this expectation, due to the violation of mirror symmetry.

> The failure of mirror image reflection to be a symmetry of laws of nature is an embarrassment for the relationist account... for as it stands that account does not have the analytical resources for expressing the lawlike left-right asymmetry for the analogue of Kant's hand standing alone. Putting some 20th century words into Kant's mouth, let it be imagined that the first created process is a $\pi^- + p \to \Lambda^0 + K^0$, $\Lambda^0 \to \pi^- + p$ decay (Ibid).

If this were the first created process of particle transformation in the adduced example of weak interactions of elementary particles, it would be mirror asymmetrical in some initial way, just as Kant insisted that a lone hand would be either left or right, even there is no other material object in the universe in order this intrinsic quality of the hand to be ascertained in relation to it. The inner difference between incongruent mirror objects must be accounted for only by their relations to absolute space, which is the first ground of the possibility of the composition of their material structure.

This original idea of Kant is adopted by contemporary scientific knowledge, although put into a new and broader theoretical conception of space. Physicists do not speak today of the reality of Newton's three-dimensional absolute space, in which Kant has sought "some sort of pervasive asymmetry", but of the reality of the four-dimensional space-time, to be responsible for parity violation. But the idea has been kept the same regarding the reality of space-time in relation to "the compositeness of matter". Thus for instance it is said that "neutrinos are always left-handed, anti-neutrinos always right-handed".

With this conclusion in mind, together with that of paragraph (2.1), I dare say that my task in defending the central claim (C_1) of this chapter is accomplished. Yet some words have to be added, if we look back at the beginning of this paragraph.

I have drawn the reader's attention there on the fact that symmetries in nature are important, since they provide the validity of the known laws of conservation. But why some symmetries, as parity for example, are sometimes violated, or in Feynman's words, why is nature so nearly symmetrical? As we saw, his metaphorical answer is a confession that we don't know why. But we know, at least for now, that a triple combination of symmetries that are broken in isolation, or in couples, is not violated for the material processes in the world. This triple combination is known as *CPT-invariance*. It consists of three separate symmetrical transformations: charge conjugation (C), or a replacement of all particles in a physical system with their corresponding anti-particles; parity reversal (P), or a mirror reflection of the system in space; and time reversal (T). CPT-invariance means that any physical system will have the same behavior, and no difference will be observed after the above transformations were accomplished. It is said that the system is invariant under the combined CPT transformation,[18] or has CPT symmetry.

We may not know, together with R. Feynman, why one of the symmetries – (P) – is violated in the sphere of weak interactions, but we may say, prompted by Kant, that space-time has a reality of its own, which has something to do with the "compositeness of matter", so that physical processes stay invariant with respect to the combined CPT transformation. Parity a-symmetry is "compensated" by the other two transformations, and maybe, vice versa: each of the three symmetries is dependent on the other two. Thus at a higher level, at which the three symmetries are combined, though broken in separation, they restore together the symmetry of nature.

REFERENCES

Barrow, John D. and Frank J. Tipler. 1986. *The Anthropic Cosmological Principle*. Oxford, New York: Oxford University Press.

Bernecker, Sven. 2010. "Kant on Spatial Orientation." *European Journal of Philosophy* Vol. 20, N4: 519–533.

Caruso F., R. Moreira Xavier. 1996. "On Kant's First Insight into

---

[18]CPT-invariance is presented by the CPT-theorem which states that any Lorentz invariant local quantum field theory with a Hermitian Hamiltonian must possess CPT symmetry.

the Problem of Dimensionality and Its Physical Foundations." *CBPF-NF*-079/96. arXiv:0907.3531 [physics.hist-ph]

Feynman, Richard P., Leighton R. B., Sands M. 1964. *The Feynman Lectures on Physics.* Reading, Massachusetts. Palo Alto. London: Addison-Wesley Publishing Company, Inc.

Frederick, Robert E. 1991. "Introduction to the Argument of 1768." In *The Philosophy of Right and Left. Incongruent Counterparts and the Nature of Space*, edited by James Van Cleve and Robert E. Frederick, 1-14. Dordrecht / Boston / London: Kluwer Academic Publishers.

Gardner, Martin. 1991. "The Fourth Dimension." In *The Philosophy of Right and Left. Incongruent Counterparts and the Nature of Space*, edited by James Van Cleve and Robert E. Frederick, 61-74. Dordrecht / Boston / London: Kluwer Academic Publishers.

Kant, Immanuel. 1929. "Thoughts on the True Estimation of Living Forces." In *Kant's Inaugural Dissertation and Early Writings on Space*, translated by John Handyside, 3-15. Chicago: Open Court Pub. Co. (Hyperion reprint edition, 1994)

Kant, Immanuel. 1929a. "Dissertation on the Form and Principles of the Sensible and Intelligible World." In *Kant's Inaugural Dissertation and Early Writings on Space*, translated by John Handyside, 35-85. Chicago: Open Court Pub. Co. (Hyperion reprint edition, 1994)

Kant, Immanuel. 1991. "On the First Ground of the Distinction of Regions in Space." In *The Philosophy of Right and Left. Incongruent Counterparts and the Nature of Space*, edited by James Van Cleve and Robert E. Frederick, 27-33. Dordrecht / Boston / London: Kluwer Academic Publishers.

Mühlhölzer, Felix. 1992. "Das Phänomen der inkongruenten Gegenstücke aus Kantische und heutiger Sicht." *Kant-Studien* Band 83: 436-453.

Palmquist, Stephen. 2010. "The Kantian Grounding of Einstein's Worldview: (I) The Early Influence of Kant's System of Perspectives." *Polish Journal of Philosophy* Vol. 4, N 1: 45-64.

Remnant, Peter. 1991. "Incongruent Counterparts and Absolute Space." In *The Philosophy of Right and Left. Incongruent Counterparts and the Nature of Space*, edited by James Van Cleve and Robert

E. Frederick, 51-59. Dordrecht / Boston / London: Kluwer Academic Publishers.

Schönfeld, Martin. 2000. *The Philosophy of the Young Kant. The Precritical Project.* Oxford University Press.

Severo, Rogério Passos. 2005. "Three Remarks on the Interpretation of Kant on Incongruent Counterparts." *Kantian Review* Vol. 9 (special anniversary issue): 30-57.

Van Cleve, James. 1991. "Right, Left, and the Fourth Dimension." In *The Philosophy of Right and Left. Incongruent Counterparts and the Nature of Space*, edited by James Van Cleve and Robert E. Frederick, 203-234. Dordrecht / Boston / London: Kluwer Academic Publishers.

Wittgenstein, Ludwig. 1961. *Tractatus Logico-Philosophicus.* (Edited by A. J. Ayer) London: Routledge & Kegan Paul.

3 Paradigmatic Criticisms of Kant's Transcendental Conception of Space and Time

Two types of criticism of Kant's transcendental conception of space and time are presented and analyzed in this chapter. While the reason for the first one is easily disclosed to be a conceptual misunderstanding, the second type is called "enduring criticism of Kant's transcendental conception of space and time". It is organized around the contention that Kant's conception involves the assumption about the validity of the three-dimensional Euclidean geometry for the physical world. A reconstruction of this type of criticism is suggested for the purpose of showing its irrelevance.

Key words: conceptual misunderstanding, pure and physical geometry, intuitive geometry.

The claim (C_2) is the main subject of this chapter. This claim states that paradigmatic criticisms of Kant's transcendental conception of space and time stem out of misunderstandings, underpinned by philosophers and scientists who are visible figures in their respective cultural (and ideological) circles (see the *Introduction*).

In paragraph (3.1) two types of criticism are presented. The first one is of a general philosophical character, sometimes displaying an ideological backing. Leaving the latter aside, the criticism is based on a non-intriguing conceptual misunderstanding. The second type is called "enduring criticism of Kant's transcendental conception of space and time". It is far more interesting and more intricate than the first one, and is organized around the contention that Kant's conception involves the assumption about the validity of the three-dimensional

Euclidean geometry for the physical world. Paragraph (3.2) presents a reconstruction of this second type of criticism. Then it is broadly analyzed and its irrelevance is set out.

3.1 What the Criticisms of Kant's Transcendental Conception of Space and Time Amount to?

Prevailing criticisms against Kant's transcendental conception of space and time can be referred to two main types[19].

The first type of criticism is a standard reaction of realistically-minded philosophers[20] to any conception of space and time that is found to be a subjectivist one. This type of criticism has a general philosophical character. And insofar as Kant's transcendental aesthetic is estimated by some such philosophers to be a piece of subjectivism, it should be criticized from this point of view.

This kind of criticism may take the form of a staunch position when some ideological prejudice is also involved. Thus, in the near past, representatives of dialectical materialism displayed a firm negative reaction to any philosophy that contains the term "idealism" in its name. Such a position is quite understandable with respect to conceptions within the field of subjective and of objective idealism in the strict Engelsean terminology. It could be demonstrated, of course, that transcendental idealism does not fall into any one of the idealistic groups of philosophies just mentioned. This fact notwithstanding, in the Marxist tradition transcendental aesthetic was often referred to subjective idealism. And because "Kant's teaching about space and time is subjective and idealistic" (Karapetyan 1958, 160), it has to be rejected.[21]

Ideological exhortations in this case, however, do not contribute

---

[19] For the first time these types of criticism were presented in (Stefanov 2003, 170-173).

[20] Not in the sense of Kant's empirical realism.

[21] According to the same author who presented otherwise an interesting voluminous study of the philosophy of the Königsberg thinker: "The real basis of Kant's phenomenalism, and of his subjective idealism in general, is the teaching about the ideality or subjectiveness of time and space. All efforts of Kant to draw a line between himself and the resolute idealism of Berkeley are unsuccessful, since he builds his transcendental idealism namely upon the teaching about the ideality of time and space" (Karapetyan 1958, 155-6).

much for the considered type of criticism, namely for its general and principal character. The criticism is standard as a motivation – a philosophical position, in our case Kant's conception of space and time, is being declined because it is in contradiction to another one, based on a widespread form of philosophical realism, assuming space and time to possess an objective ontological status.[22] And now, *the misunderstanding at the base of the considered type of criticism* can easily be disclosed. It is rooted in the firm clinging on the side of the criticizing realists to their own notion of space and time. They abandon (or do not even take into account) Kant's transcendental context, laying at the same time their own notion into assertions that are constitutive for this same context. But a realist (a materialist) notion of space and time has quite different a meaning from the transcendental one, and if someone has actually set as a precondition a materialist notion of space and time in a typically Kantian assertion, then she would have come upon a subjectivist claim.

Kantian space and time are neither noumenal essences, nor objective relations, because, according to him, they compose the conditions for the very possibility of human experience. If Kant would have contended that space and time, taken as some *external* givenness to the knowing subject or as *objective* relations among directly knowable things, are *subjective*, then he would have produced not a sheer subjective-idealistic claim, but rather a conspicuous inconsistent declaration.

Kant's transcendental conception of space and time will be briefly considered in the next paragraph. But it becomes clear that one may not blame Kant for being a subjectivist, which he really is not. Subjectivism as a label is a "correct" one for transcendental aesthetic only in a very specific sense, namely that space and time *as pure intuitions* are found to be "with" the perceiving subject. And in this quality, indeed, there is no way for space and time to be externally objective[23], even if a Kantian would hypothetically presume the existence of some "transcendent" space and time encompassing things in themselves. Such presumption has been considered by proponents of the so called "neglected alternative argument" that will not be a matter of

---

[22]In this sense space and time could either be taken as autonomous entities, or as objective relations among physical objects within the world.

[23]Space and time in a transcendental context are objective, indeed, but in quite another sense, in so far as they are constitutive for the objects and their relations within human experience.

interest here.[24] The only "criticism", which then might be addressed towards Kant is, why he puts just his transcendental meaning in the representations of space and time, and evades their realist meaning as ontological concepts (having in mind that this meaning was not foreign to him in his so called pre-critical creative period). However, this question can play the role of a critical argument, just as much as the belief that doing metaphysics must follow ready-made conceptual schemes, can serve as a revelation.

The second type of criticism against Kant's transcendental aesthetic is also rooted in a misunderstanding, whose argumentative structure will be presented in the next paragraph. However, in contrast to the just considered one, it exhibits the feature of a telling criticism, since it explores the inherent geometrical characteristics of the proposed space, and is based upon the post-Kantian development of mathematics, physics, and cosmology. What is this type of criticism about?

Kant puts forward an original *philosophical* conception of space and time, or *the* space and *the* time. By inserting a definite article in front of the last nouns I would like to point to their one-ness, or uniqueness, having also in mind that the pure intuitions expressed by them are referent to the sphere of the knowing subject; and there one can hardly expect, even less postulate, the presence of *different* spaces and times. The Königsberg thinker brings out the cognitive role and functions of space and time, and not so much their geometrical characteristics. But if we ought to involve mathematical terminology, then Kantian space should be qualified as being three-dimensional and flat (i.e. having no curvature), or as three-dimensional Euclidean space. Time is one-dimensional and continuous.

This being the case, the objections of too many authors (philosophers and scientists), roughly speaking, since the beginning of the twentieth century onwards, are based on the fact of the collection of a nosegay of *non-Euclidean geometries*. Some of them – such authors argue – could represent the features of physical space and time in a better way than is within the possibility of Euclidean geometry, which is constructive only for the ontology of the classical Newtonian picture of the world. Even a sparing critical conclusion, which is alluded to, is that Kant's commitment to only Euclidean geometry is a manifestation of a methodological improvidence. Such objections generate what I called at the beginning of this chapter "*an enduring*

---

[24]For this argument see for example (Vaihinger 1922, 134-151).

criticism of Kant's transcendental conception of space and time". It was, though not initiated, but reinforced by the overlapping criticisms of Kant made by R. Carnap, H. Reichenbach, A. Grünbaum, and K. Popper.

Pavel Florensky, a connoisseur in the thematic field of space and time both in positive science and fine arts, wrote in 1924, that

> one hundred years ago N. I. Lobachevski stated the resolute anti-Kantian thought, which remained then only as a bold dictum, namely that different phenomena of the physical world take place in different spaces, and are, therefore subordinated to the corresponding laws of those spaces (Florensky 1993, 5).

The presence of "different spaces" (not of sub-spaces of one space) is at variance with the Kantian assumption of only one space. The expression here means physical spaces with different properties, convenient for the "different phenomena of the physical world" to take place in those different spaces. P. Florensky himself maintains the view that *geometry is an empirical science.* The geometry of space is determined, according to him, by the field of forces and the latter, vice versa, by geometry (Ibid, 7).

Recording rightly that Kantian time and space are neither self-subsistent entities, nor empirical generalizations, but *a priori* forms of sensory perception, Milič Čapek still insists that

> Kant's view of time was as Newtonian as his view of space... the Newtonian model of the universe with both its components – Euclidian space and mathematically continuous time – is beyond the danger of being challenged by *any* further experience. No wonder that quite a number of *neo-Kantians were not happy when this bold prediction of their master clashed with the new trends in physics and geometry.*[25]

The clear conclusion from this quotation is that because of the clash of Kant's conception (allegedly predicting the validity of Euclidean geometry to the physical world) "with the new trends in physics and geometry", it must be rejected. However, it is a necessary condition for a conception "to clash" with another one, that both of them have

---

[25](Čapek 1976, XXXVI), my italics.

the same cognitive pretention, or possess the same epistemological status. To this effect Čapek builds his reasoning *on a hidden, but a key premise*. This is the premise that Kant's conception of "Euclidean space and mathematically continuous time", through the Newtonian model of the universe, bears the same epistemological status as that of "the new trends in physics and geometry", stating that the geometry of physical space-time is *not* Euclidean. And because these new trends exploit theoretical models of the spatio-temporal structure of the universe different from the Newtonian model, the Kantian base of the latter should be abandoned.

I shall try to explain in 3.2 that this is a misleading premise. It is rooted in the conviction that *Kant prescribes a true geometry to the world, and this is the Euclidean geometry*. A lot of scientists and philosophers share this conviction; and it stays at the base of the enduring criticism of Kant's transcendental conception of space and time. As David Deutsch puts it:

> It is just possible (though I do not believe it) that Euclidean geometry or Aristotelian logic are somehow built into the structure of our brains, as the philosopher Immanuel Kant believed. But that would not logically imply that they were true (Deutsch 1997, 254).

There are far more trenchant assessments of Kant's conception to declare that it is merely false. Zucker contends for instance that such "blunders" as are his *a priori* arguments in support of Euclidean geometry, absolute space and Newtonian mechanics, "spell the collapse of Kant's entire attempt" (Zucker 1969, 480).

The considered type of criticism is shared by philosophers and scientists, expressing different attitudes towards Kant's philosophical heritage. In this whole spectrum of related opinions I am mostly interested in the argumentation of such thinkers who, according to claim (C$_2$), "are visible figures in their respective cultural (and ideological) circles". The quoted authors are of this kind, I believe, and undoubtedly, such are *Rudolf Carnap* and *Hans Reichenbach*, who have proved for a long time their methodological competence and creative capacity. Moreover, their critical attitude towards Kant's conception of space and time has become paradigmatic, or at least very popular, within contemporary philosophy of science. It suffices to mention Adolf Grünbaum's famous book *Philosophical Problems of Space and Time*, in which the reader is notified – as something well established – that

Reichenbach made a particularly telling contribution
to the disintegration of the Kantian *metrical* a priori of
visual space by showing that such intuitive compulsion as
inheres in the Euclideanism of that space derives from facts
of logic in which the Kantian interpretation cannot find a
last refuge...[26]

My interest in the criticism these philosophers have launched is
also motivated by the fact that their own conceptions of space and
time seem acceptable or at least comprehensible for thinkers who are
tending towards philosophical realism. This means here that when
displaying my dissention with the statements of R. Carnap and H.
Reichenbach, I *am not* going to criticize neither *their own* conceptions
of space and time, nor the scientific status and applicability of non-
Euclidean geometries. I shall make an attempt instead at showing
their misunderstanding of Kant's transcendental viewpoint, and thus
to complete my argumentation in support of (C$_2$).

3.2 The Irrelevance of the Enduring Criticism

Having been guided by his respect towards the Königsberg thinker,
Rudolf Carnap even makes an attempt at mitigating his otherwise
clear criticism of Kant's conception:

Kant should not be blamed for his error because, in his
day, non-Euclidean geometry had not been discovered. *It
was not possible for him to think about geometry in any
other way.* In fact, throughout the entire nineteenth century, except for a few bold individuals, such as Gauss,
Riemann, and Heimholtz, *even mathematicians took this
Kantian point of view for granted.*[27]

But has Kant made an error? After acquaintance with Reichenbach's and Carnap's reasoning, the answer may well be positive for a
reader not tempted by Kant's philosophy.

---

[26](Grünbaum 1974, 154) It seems contemporary scientists like David Deutsch
uncritically endorse the quoted evaluation, so that to declare as we have seen, that
even if Euclidean geometry was "somehow built into the structure of our brains,
as the philosopher Immanuel Kant believed", *that would not logically imply that it
was true.*

[27](Carnap 1966, 181), my italics.

Let us see now what the error, imposed on Kant, consists in? One may easily conclude, even from what has been said up to now, that the error consists in postulating the truth of Euclidean geometry for the natural world (mainly on the base of the uniqueness of the visual space and the perceived time), and in thus not admitting the possibility of even essential corrections, coming from future theoretical and/or empirical scientific discoveries. Kant was a child of his Newtonian epoch, and (even he) could not rise over its conceptual framework. "It was not possible for him to think about geometry in any other way." But the fruitful development of mathematical investigations during the 19th, and especially during the 20th century, have opened the possibility for the construction – in a non-contradictory manner – of various mathematical spaces, based on non-Euclidean axiomatic. The axioms, or the initial statements of formal constructions, *cease to be looked upon as obvious truths any longer*, as the recognized tradition has required for ages, since ancient times till the middle of the 19th century. Hans Reichenbach (1958, 5-6) clearly explains that

> for geometry as a mathematical science, there is no problem concerning the truth of the axioms. This apparently unsolvable problem turns out to be a pseudo-problem. The axioms are not true or false, but arbitrary statements. It was soon discovered that the other axioms could be treated in the same way as the axiom of the parallels... The discussion of this statement leads away from mathematics; as a question about a property of the physical world, it is a *physical* question, not a *mathematical* one. This distinction, which grew out of the discovery of non-Euclidean geometry, has a fundamental significance: it divides the problem of space into two parts; the problem of mathematical space is recognized as different from the problem of physical space.

R. Carnap's specification of Kant's error goes just along this line of reasoning:

> Today, it is easy to see the source of Kant's error. It was a failure to realize that there are two essentially different kinds of geometry – one mathematical, the other physical (Carnap 1966, 181).

Mathematical geometry is an abstract deductive system, based on axioms "that do not have to be interpreted by reference to any existing world". In this sense *it is a pure construction*. "Physical geometry, on the other hand, is concerned with the application of pure geometry to the world."[28]

R. Carnap goes still further in his critique of Kant's philosophy. After a presentation of the distinction drawn by Kant between analytical and synthetical judgments, he declines the answer to the central problem of Kant's transcendental approach: do synthetical *a priori* judgments exist and how they are possible? As opposed to Kant, Carnap raises the doctrine that there are no such judgments in mathematics and one can still less imagine how they are possible in a natural science like physics.[29] Mathematical geometry, according to Carnap, refers to pure mathematics. As a pure science it is really apprioristic (i.e., no statements with an empirical content are interwoven in it), but this geometry is not synthetical, it is analytical. This is so, because mathematical geometry is a deductive system whose axioms are provided with no interpretation at all, that could refer them to some fragment of the existing world.

> Once this distinction between pure and physical geometry is understood, it becomes clear how Kant's belief, and the beliefs of almost all nineteenth-century philosophers, involved a fundamental confusion between two fields of quite different character (Carnap 1966, 182-3).

Now, it is easy the coinciding criticisms of Reichenbach and Carnap against "Kant's belief" to be reconstructed. The criticism rests upon the following lucid theses:

(1) Two types of geometry must be clearly differentiated – mathematical (pure), and physical.

(2) Kant does not make the distinction (1), and to this effect he does not admit the possibility some other, different from the Euclidean geometry, to be true of the physical space.

(3) The scientific growth of mathematics has given birth to non-Euclidean geometries, and that of physics and cosmology – to Einstein's general theory of relativity, which establishes the validity of an essentially non-Euclidean geometry – of the Riemannian geometry.

---

[28]The distinction between mathematical and physical geometry is cogently explained by R. Carnap in his book (1966, 181-183).

[29]Cf. (Carnap 1966, ch. 18). He also clearly states elsewhere that "It is the contention of construction theory that there are no such things as the "synthetic judgments a priori" which are essential for Kant's approach to epistemological problems" (Carnap 1967, 176).

(4) It follows from (2) and (3) that Kant has made an error.

To all appearances the immediacy of this criticism has convinced a lot of contemporary authors to accept it as a cogent argument against Kant. This fact is valid not only for western analytic philosophy, but for the eastern dialectic-materialist context, as well. "Why was Kant wrong?" This familiar question was raised by V. L. Hramova in her book about the relation between theory and experiment in relativistic physics (Hramova 1974). The direct answer is as follows: "The trouble lies in the fact that he had not differentiated the two kinds of geometry – the mathematical and the physical one" (Ibid, 173). The same critical argument stands in one of the most authoritative university textbooks in philosophy of science of our days, prepared by Martin Curd and Jan Cover. One can read there that "whether Euclidean geometry is true of space is an empirical matter, not something we can know a priori as Kant and Frege had thought", since after the success of Einstein's general theory of relativity we have to distinguish between the two types of geometry, mentioned above (Curd and Cover 1998, 370). Moreover, M. Čapek tries to convince us that Kant

> *would be equally shocked* by the Riemannian geometry as by Lemaître's and Gamow's cosmogonies assuming the finiteness of the cosmic past bounded by the initial 'zero-time'.[30]

The reconstructed criticism, as it is seen, has become an enduring criticism of Kant's transcendental conception of space and time. I'll try to show that this is an irrelevant criticism.

I have two reasons not to express any doubts about thesis (1). Since Hermann Minkowski ascertained the four-dimensional pseudo-Euclidean character of physical space-time in 1908, and especially since the creation of the general theory of relativity (and the methodological discussions engendered by it), the so called problem of the *complementarity* of geometry and physics has become much debated in the philosophy of science. In fact, this is a problem about the choice of a convenient mathematical structure – a geometrical space having definite metrical and topological properties – which can describe in a feasible manner the thing, accepted by contemporary scientists to be "the real physical space-time".

The second and essential reason to leave (1) without further comment, is the following. If the thesis is taken to be false, then the critical

---

[30](Čapek 1971, 43), my italics.

arguments (2-4) against Kant lose their validity, and thus my task is accomplished. What I am interested in here, however, is to show that theses (2-4) are an *irrelevant* criticism of Kant, admitting the truth of thesis (1).

Statement (4) is a formal conclusion, bearing a critical charge only if arguments (2-3) are valid. Being a statement of fact, (3) can be taken as unproblematic. So, *(2) proves to be the focal thesis that bears the burden of the criticism.* This is why my aim here is to show why thesis (2) is an irrelevant piece of criticism against Kant's transcendental conception of space and time.

An overture to my criticism of the critical thesis (2) is the elucidation of the fact that the pretention of (1) is not a problem of Kant as an author of his first *Critique* and of the *Prolegomena*. The distinction between pure and physical geometry *stays thematically outside of his transcendental aesthetic*, no matter how fruitful this distinction has proved to be later for physical science. Kant's aim for the introduction of the aesthetical representations of space and time is epistemological, not physical. He is not facing the problem about the description of space and time as having an independent existence of the perceiving subject, i.e. about their description as some objective entities or relations, standing against the cognizing spirit. And in so far as the very idea about distinguishing mathematical from physical geometry does not fit Kant's philosophical transcendental setting, then one could hardly speak of a "fundamental confusion" which Kant has allegedly made "between two fields of quite different character".

But (2) may still be a critical argument against Kant, if, as the thesis goes, "he does not admit the possibility some other, different from the Euclidean geometry, to be true of the physical space". This criticism presupposes that Kant ascribes a primary validity to three-dimensional Euclidean geometry as being the geometry of the physical space, and thus suggests a *theoretical ontology for the space structure of the natural world*. (Needless to say, then Kant – as M. Čapek insists – "*would be equally shocked* by the Riemannian geometry as by... cosmogonies assuming the finiteness of the cosmic past bounded by the initial 'zero-time'.") Reichenbach's interpretation seems to be of this kind. According to him, the Kantian doctrine

> contends that an innate property of the human mind, the ability of visualization, *demands that we adhere to Euclidean geometry*. In the same way as a certain self-evidence compels us to believe the laws of arithmetic, a

> visual self-evidence *compels us to believe in the validity of Euclidean geometry.* It can be shown that this self-evidence is not based on logical grounds.[31]

H. Reichenbach substantiates the last statement by proving a theorem, which stands at the heart of the already mentioned problem of the complementarity between geometry and physics, presented in his book as *the principle of the relativity of geometry.* The epistemological moral of this theorem is that we cannot meaningfully speak of *any* geometry of space to be the *true* geometry. This is so, because only a *combination* between geometry and a universal field of force can produce empirically verifiable claims about physical reality. Thus a freedom exists for our choice of a spatial geometry, and this is stated by the principle of the relativity of geometry. With this principle in mind, it is easy to see why the preference for Euclidean geometry as the true geometry of physical space, imposed by a visual self-evidence, is void of any logical argument.

Reichenbach's view, followed by many philosophers of science, is (at least formally) beyond any doubt, with the exception of the *type of apriorism* imputed to Kant. In fact, Reichenbach raises two separate claims:

(R_1) The Kantian doctrine "contends that an innate property of the human mind, the ability of visualization, *demands that we adhere to Euclidean geometry*".

(R_2) The same innate property, taken as a visual self-evidence, "*compels us to believe in the validity of Euclidean geometry*".

Though claims (R_1) and (R_2) may seem to be very near in content, they are *different* claims. One may well take (R_1) to be a correct interpretation of "the Kantian doctrine", rejecting at the same time the pretention of (R_2).

There is a plausible explanation why "the ability of visualization demands that we adhere to Euclidean geometry". In a transcendental context the ability of visualization as "an innate property of the human mind" is the pure sensuous intuition of the external sense, called space by Kant. As a pure form of sensibility space supplies the mere form of the phenomena (Kant 1966, 22-3, *CPR*, A: 20, B: 34), which means that *through space* the extensions of the objects and their mutual relations are given to us as empirical intuitions. And if space, being "a necessary representation *a priori*, forming the very foundation of

---

[31](Reichenbach 1958, 32), my italics.

all external intuitions" (Kant 1966, 24, *CPR*, A: 24, B: 38) displays Euclidean features, then we must certainly adhere to Euclidean geometry, since all objects of experience, or, in other words, *the world for us*, is spatially organized on the base of this geometry (notwithstanding what kind of principally unknown characteristics things in themselves might possess).

Space, as a pure intuition (reine Anschauung) is all-pervasive, and this role of space can be seen when the answer is being sought to the question: "why are non-Euclidean figures not possible to be perceived?" The answer is successfully discussed by David Sherry who turns the philosophical attention to Kant's image forming synthesis, which is one and the same both for geometrical constructions and for perceptions of empirical objects. He brings out Kant's aprioristic position, that "we construct objects of experience according to the same principles by which we construct mathematical objects" (Sherry 1999, 35). It becomes clear now why non-Euclidean figures are ruled out as impossible perceptions: "the same formative synthesis, by which we construct a triangle in imagination, should be identical with that which we exercise in the apprehension of a phenomenon, in order to make an empirical concept of it" (Kant 1966, 174, *CPR*, A: 224, B: 271).[32] The world, as is given to us, as well as our imaginative constructions of possible representations, display Euclidean features, and to this effect we adhere to Euclidean geometry.

So, (R_1) may be taken as an arguable claim.

Let us turn now to the pretention of (R_2). What this claim states, is that our ability of visualization, i.e. space as an *a priori* form of sensibility, "compels us to believe in the validity of Euclidean geometry". This is a *strong type of apriorism*, which admits that our innate ability of visualization provides us with knowledge about the real spatial characteristics of the world. If (R_2) is a veridical claim, then the formal result of Reichenbach about the absence of logical priority of any geometry whatsoever to be true of the world, would represent a strong critical argument against this type of apriorism.

Curious as it may seem, a prominent philosopher like Karl Popper, with all his great methodological respect for Kant, shares some part of

---

[32]Non-Euclidean spaces cannot be visualized (at least by humans), i.e. they do not underlie our ability of visualization, in the sense that we do not acquire the appearances of objects *through* them, although two-dimensional samples of non-Euclidean spaces can be *modeled within* the three-dimensional Euclidean space. Thus, by the surface of a sphere a two-dimensional Riemannian space is being presented in a three-dimensional Euclidean space.

this Reichenbachean position. I find the fact to be curious, since as far as I know, Popper has never been intellectually influenced by Reichenbach. Anyhow, he (also) writes that Kant has made an error, although this error detracts in no way from his magnificent achievement.

> What was his error? As I have said, Kant, like almost all philosophers and epistemologists right into the twentieth century, was convinced that Newton's theory was *true*... It was an unavoidable error – unavoidable, that is, before Einstein (Popper 1989, 190-191).

The "error" that Reichenbach and Popper impute to Kant comes out of the misleading presupposition that the pure forms of sensibility supply us with *a priori knowledge* about the spatial and temporal structure of the physical world as it is. Going back to Reichenbach, this is expressed in the alleged *validation* of the Euclidean geometry, which is an ontological interpretation. As for Popper, the same interpretation of Kant's apriorism is specified by his declaration about (the alleged) Kant's conviction of the truth of Newton's theory, based on the Euclidean features of absolute space and absolute time. I may also add here M. Čapek's exhortation that "Kant's view of time was as Newtonian as his view of space" (3.1, fn. 25).

However, *Kant's apriorism is not of this strong type*. Kant's critical standpoint, I argue, prevents him from establishing the truth of a geometry, be it Euclidean, or not, being guided by some unclear "innate property of the human mind", as Reichenbach puts it. In fact, such an innate property of the mind shows a cognitive kinship with inborn ideas, in so far as in an aprioristic mode it provides knowledge for the true nature of the physical space. Kant's apriorism is transcendental, i.e. it has an epistemological pretention to reach the answer how knowledge is possible, and does not have an ontological pretention for any *a priori* knowledge about physical space and time. For Kant

> Space does not represent any quality of objects by themselves, or objects in their relation to one another; i.e. space does not represent any determination which is inherent in the objects themselves, and would remain, even if all subjective conditions of intuition were removed... Space is nothing but the form of all phenomena of the external senses; it is the subjective condition of our sensibility, without which no external intuition is possible for us (Kant 1966, 26, *CPR*, A: 26, B: 42).

Time also, according to Kant, is not something existing by itself, and is not inherent in things as an objective determination of them, but is the form of the internal sense, of our intuition of ourselves (Ibid, 30-31, *CPR*, A: 32-33, B: 49).

All this means that under the aesthetical terms of space and time Kant understands pure *a priori* forms of sensibility, which make possible the very possession of any empirical intuition. It is well known that knowledge acquisition is hardly possible without sensuous intuitions, or to remind the famous Kant's dictum: "Thoughts without contents are empty, intuitions without concepts are blind" (Ibid, 45, *CPR*, A: 51, B: 75). Space and time, however, being forms of every intuition whatsoever when sensation (Empfindung) is present, are at the very "base" of sensibility (Sinnlichkeit). This is why space and time are referent to the cognizing spirit: they are *pure* intuitions prior to any experience, which make possible the arrangement of "the matter of experience" into a clear cut *empirical* intuition. Only in this way do objects of experience become possible.

In a nutshell, these are the basic elements of Kant's aesthetical apriorism, concerning the cognitive role of space and time as necessary forms (accepting the matter) of every phenomenon. Now, it becomes clear, I suppose, that Reichenbach and Carnap criticize not this original Kantian position, but some not well defined, yet naïve type of apriorism. Kant's apriorism is entirely transcendental, while the criticized one is "naturalized" by introducing some innate tendency, compelling us to believe in the validity of Euclidean geometry for the physical space and time, although they (can) really submit to a non-Euclidean geometry. It is one thing to say that space and time are the *a priori* conditions for the very cognitive possession of objects of experience, and quite another thing to insist that an innate property of the human mind leads to the acceptance of Euclidean geometry as *the* geometry of the physical world, *and thus to introduce a definite ontology for it* (as is Popper's contention for instance about Kant's conviction that Newton's theory is *true*).

Now, I can make the conclusion that *the enduring criticism (1-4) of Carnap and Reichenbach, embraced by other philosophers and scientists as well, is an irrelevant criticism.*

Indeed, it was demonstrated that the distinction (1), no matter how plausible, is not a problem for transcendental aesthetic. Thesis (2) bears all the critical burden of the argumentation (1-4), but it has proved to be an irrelevant piece of criticism. The reason is that the thesis exploits a specific misunderstanding, involving an irrelevant interpretation of Kant's transcendental apriorism. So, the enduring criticism as a whole proves to be irrelevant.

With this conclusion, together with the conclusion about the failure of the first type of criticism (see (3.1)), *the central claim (C₂) of the present chapter is defended.*

Before finishing this paragraph, however, I have to add *two relevant remarks* to the otherwise irrelevant criticism reconstructed by theses (1-4).

Let me begin with the first remark. As we have already seen, the benevolent critics of Kant attract a historical explanation, as an excuse, for the alleged "error" made by him. It involves the fact that non-Euclidean geometry had not yet been discovered in the days when Kant was creating his transcendental philosophy. This is a good reason for Carnap to maintain that "Kant should not be blamed for his error", and for Popper to say that "it was an unavoidable error – unavoidable, that is, before Einstein". Carnap convincingly adds also that "*it was not possible for him to think about geometry in any other way*", when "even mathematicians took this Kantian point of view for granted".[33]

Notwithstanding its benevolence, the adduced explanation of what was thought to be Kant's "error" omits a fact, probably unknown for the critics. It is true, of course, that non-Euclidean geometries had not been constructed as formal systems in the days when Kant was creating his transcendental metaphysics, but as we already know from (2.1), pre-critical Kant had admitted the possibility of extensions depicted by geometries different from the three-dimensional Euclidean geometry one century before non-Euclidean geometries were discovered. To this effect the contention that "it was not possible for him to think about geometry in any other way" *is not correct.* In its turn this fact runs counter thesis (2), that Kant does not admit (or, better say, had never admitted) the possibility some other, different from the Euclidean geometry, to be true of the physical space.

The second remark concerns the fact that the critics of Kant's transcendental conception readily uphold (1) and (2) as basic claims of the considered enduring criticism. But is (1) an exhaustive distinction between two types of geometry? Laurence BonJour's speculative answer to this question is rather negative. He asks whether we have an intuitive grasp of the notion of straightness that is independent of the identification of straight lines with physical phenomena, e.g. with

---

[33]See fn. 27.

a light ray (BonJour 1998, 223-4). And then argues that

> If we have such an intuitive conception of straightness, then the usual discussions that turn on a dichotomy between a "pure geometry" that is merely an uninterpreted formal system and an "applied geometry" or "physical geometry" that depends on the identification of straight lines with physical phenomena omit a crucial alternative: a geometry that is neither merely formal nor in this sense physical, but rather reflects our intuitive notion of straightness and its implications (Ibid, 224).

Of what kind is this alternative geometry, let me call it "intuitive geometry", reflecting our intuitive notion of straightness? It is just the geometry by which we visualize objects of experience through the pure intuition called space by Kant. This is the geometry through which nature is perceived by us, since Kant defines nature "as the sum total of the objects of experience" (Kant 1966, xxxiv, *CPR*, B: xix), or as "the coherence of phenomena in their existence, according to necessary rules, that is, laws" (Kant 1966, 169, *CPR*, A: 216, B: 263). Having in mind that the cognitive possession by humans of any object of experience and of the relations among phenomena is possible because of space as an a priori sensuous intuition, it becomes clear that the intuitive geometry is the Euclidean geometry. Only in this *transcendental* sense Euclidean geometry is valid for the natural world – *in the sense of intuitive geometry.*

REFERENCES

BonJour, Laurence. 1998. *In Defense of Pure Reason. A Rationalist Account of* A Priori *Justification.* Cambridge: Cambridge University Press.

Čapek, Milič. 1971. *Bergson and Modern Physics. A Reinterpretation and Re-Evaluation.* Dordrecht: D. Reidel.

Čapek, Milič. 1976. "Introduction." In *The Concepts of Space and Time. Their Structure and Their Development*, edited by Milič Čapek. Dordrecht: D. Reidel.

Carnap, Rudolf. 1966. *Philosophical Foundations of Physics. An Introduction to the Philosophy of Science.* New York, London: Basic Books, Inc. Publishers.

48

Carnap, Rudolf. 1967. *The Logical Structure of the World and Pseudoproblems in Philosophy*. Berkeley and Los Angeles: University of California Press.

Curd, Martin and J. A. Cover. 1998. "Commentary to ch. 3." In *Philosophy of Science. The Central Issues*, edited by Martin Curd and J. A. Cover. New York, London: W. W. Norton & Company.

Deutsch, David. 1997. *The Fabric of Reality*. Harmondsworth: Penguin Books.

Florensky, P. A. 1993. *Analysis of Spatiality and Time in Works of Pictorial and Plastic Arts* (in Russian). Moscow: Publishing Group "Progress".

Grünbaum, Adolf. 1974. *Philosophical Problems of Space and Time*. Dordrecht: D. Reidel.

Hramova, V. L. 1974. *Philosophical Analysis of the Problem about the Relation between Theory and Experiment in Relativistic Physics* (in Russian). Kiev: "Naukova Dumka".

Kant, Immanuel. 1966. *Critique of Pure Reason*. Translated by F. Max Müller. Garden City, New York: Anchor Books, Doubleday & Company, Inc.

Karapetyan, A. A. 1958. *Critical Analysis of Kant's Philosophy* (in Russian). Erevan: Armenian State Publishing House.

Popper, Karl R. 1989. *Conjectures and Refutations. The Growth of Scientific Knowledge*. London: Routledge.

Reichenbach, Hans. 1958. *The Philosophy of Space and Time*. New York: Dover Publications, Inc.

Sherry, David. 1999. "Construction and *Reductio* Proof." *Kant-Studien* Band 90, Heft 1: 23-39.

Stefanov, Anguel S. 2003. "On Kant's Conception of Space and Time." In *Boston Studies in the Philosophy of Science*, vol. 236, edited by D. Ginev, 169-185. Kluwer Academic Publishers.

Vaihinger, H. 1922. *Commentar zu Kants Kritik der reinen Vernunft*, Bd. II. Stuttgart: Union Deutsche Verlagsgesellschaft.

Zucker, Francis J. 1969. "Supplementary Comments to Weizsäcker's Paper." In *Boston Studies in the Philosophy of Science*, vol. V, edited by Cohen R. and M. Wartofsky. Dordrecht: D. Reidel.

4 ARE CONCEPTS OF SPACE AND TIME COMPATIBLE WITH KANT'S TRANSCENDENTAL APPROACH?

We have seen in the previous chapter that the "enduring criticism" of Kant's transcendental conception of space and time fails, and to this effect this conception does not formally contradict contemporary physical theories. However, it stands aloof of these theories, in so far as it does not operate with concepts of space and time like those exploited by contemporary science. The aim of this chapter is to show that in spite of this fact transcendental philosophy does not set up a conceptual barrier in front of intuitive and theoretical concepts of space and time, and thus to the construction of critical ontologies of space and time.

Key words: "empirical" (intuitive) and theoretical concepts of space and time, productive faculty of imagination.

I showed in chapter 3 that the paradigmatic criticisms of Kant's transcendental conception of space and time do not hold water. The misunderstandings, staying at the base of those criticisms were revealed and critically analyzed. In so far as (the defended) claim (C_2) is correct and the so called "enduring criticism of Kant's transcendental conception" fails, it would be no surprise to say that Kant's transcendental philosophy has no need of either empirical or theoretical concepts of space and time.

The subject ideality of space and time has been thoroughly set out in the transcendental aesthetic. They are defined as pure sensuous intuitions, and *a priori* forms of sensibility, so that special concepts of space and time, as if they are objectively existing entities or relations among material objects, have no appropriate place within the conceptual framework of Kant's transcendental philosophy.

So, what have *concepts* of space and time to do with this philosophy?

Notwithstanding the irrelevance of the paradigmatic criticisms, Kant's conception of space and time can meet another type of criticism, though milder than the considered one. "Well", it can be stated, "transcendental philosophy may not formally contradict contemporary physical theories of space-time, but it does not exploit concepts of space and time, and to this effect it holds aloof of contemporary scientific knowledge."

This really seems to be a critical attitude to Kant's conception of space and time, although a defensive argument could also be raised. Indeed, the pretention of Kant's transcendental philosophy is primarily gnoseological, while the pretention of physical and cosmological theories is primarily ontological. Kant's transcendental philosophy has no need of specific concepts of space and time, simply because it chases no aim at presenting a scientific picture of the spatio-temporal structure of the universe.

Although the second part of this sentence is valid on primarily psychological grounds, but staying afar from scientific knowledge is not the best label for a philosophical system pretending to illuminate the nature of space and time (even if the opposite label be a superfluous mark for it). Removing this "negative" label is my incentive for the claim that concepts of space and time can be formed within transcendental philosophy, and my aim is to show how this is possible. This means that *I'll try to show that space and time are susceptible to conceptualization*. It is not a mere and only result of extrapolation from experience, but presupposes their aprioristic role in the very formation of experience. *Thus argumentation will be supplied for claim (C₃) which is the basic claim of this chapter*, and which states that Kant's transcendental philosophy does not set up a conceptual barrier in front of pro-empirical and theoretical concepts of space and time (see the *Introduction*).

4.1 Intuitive (Pro-Empirical) Concepts of Space and Time

Strangely enough, but Kant himself speaks, although rarely and warily, of *concepts* of space and time in connection to sensibility. When presenting the principles of a transcendental deduction in general, he writes:

> We have already become acquainted with two totally distinct classes of concepts, which nevertheless agree in this, that they both refer *a priori* to objects, namely, the concepts of space and time as forms of sensibility, and the categories as concepts of the understanding (Kant 1966, 69, *CPR*, A: 85, B: 118).

There is also a place in the *Prolegomena*, where Kant puts on a par the *conceptions* or *notions* of sensibility (space and time) and "those of the understanding", in their quality of being "pure elements (containing nothing empirical) of the human cognition":

> On investigation of the pure elements (containing nothing empirical) of the human cognition, I first succeeded, after long reflection, in distinguishing and separating with confidence the elementary conceptions of sensibility (space and time) from those of the understanding.[34]

I'll try here to suggest how space and time could acquire the use of pro-empirical (that could be better named intuitive) concepts, and in the next section to dispel the mentioned criticism that Kant's philosophy can have no touching points with theoretical constructs of space and time that are being successfully exploited by physics and cosmology.

The first step for defending the claim that space and time could be looked upon as intuitive concepts is to bring out their necessary role for the constitution of all objects of experience. The argument for this step has been provided by Kant himself, and it is worth noticing that he feels again the linguistic "pressure" to attach the word 'concept' to space and time:

---

[34](Kant 1883, §39, 71). At the corresponding place in the *Prolegomena* Paul Carus's translation is: "After long reflection on the pure elements of human knowledge (those which contain nothing empirical), I at last succeeded in distinguishing with certainty and in separating the pure elementary notions of the Sensibility (space and time) from those of the Understanding" (Kant 1997: Sect.39; 2.323). The original excerpt is: "Bei einer Untersuchung der reinen (nichts Empirisches enthaltenden) Elemente der menschlichen Erkenntniß gelang es mir allererst nach langem Nachdenken, die reinen Elementarbegriffe der Sinnlichkeit (Raum und Zeit) von denen des Verstandes mit Zuverlässigkeit zu unterscheiden und abzusondern" (Akademie edition of Kant' works: AA IV, S. 323).

Even space and time, however pure these concepts may be of all that is empirical, and however certain it is that they are represented in the mind entirely *a priori*, would lack nevertheless all objective validity, all sense and meaning, if we could not show the necessity of their use with reference to all objects of experience. Nay, their representation is a pure schema, always referring to that reproductive imagination which calls up the objects of experience, without which objects would be meaningless. The same applies to all concepts without any distinction (Kant 1966, 131, *CPR*, A: 156, B: 195).

So, though space and time have an *a priori* representational status of a "pure schema", *they are constitutive for all objects of experience.* Space and time "would lack objective validity, all sense and meaning", if they (through the reproductive faculty of imagination) did not *"call up the objects"*. Every object of experience appears as having a specific shape of its own; two or more objects are spatially related, they are perceived or imagined to coexist in some common part of space, and within some common time interval. The transcendental ideality of space and time provides the very possibility of every *empirical* intuition, and to this effect, space and time are "empirically real". Shapes and durations, spatial relations and time intervals could then be taken as belonging to a general concept of space and to a general concept of time, these concepts being formed as extrapolations out of experience: space and time are notions of what still remains when substantive bodies are driven away, or when a body is imagined to grow of volume or of temporal duration to infinity. This transformative act gives birth to space and time as utmost empirical concepts, by forming the belief that extensions of objects and their outer relations, as well as their successive temporal order do really exist, just because of the *existence* of space and time.

The second step in defense of my claim is the answer to the question "How this right-minded ontologization, no matter how much illegitimate it is from the standpoint of transcendental aesthetic, is possible?"

The only feasible answer, is that pure forms of sensibility, which make experience possible, and thus are formative for experience in "calling up its objects", can be extracted back from experience as concepts of entities, pretending to have an independent existence. In a brief remark concerning the use of the notions of cause and effect in the section about the second analogy of experience within his first *Cri-*

tique, Kant admits the way of formation of concepts by emergence out of experience, pointing once again to *the concepts* of space and time:

> The case is the same as with other pure representations *a priori* (for instance space and time), which we are only able to draw out as pure concepts from experience, because we have put them first into experience, nay, have rendered experience possible only by them (Kant 1966, 158, *CPR*, A: 196, B: 241).

Thus the mechanism of emergence of the pro-empirical, or rather say of the intuitive, concepts of space and time is but their "drawing out as pure concepts from experience, because we have put them first into experience". As cognizing subjects we have already introduced spatial and temporal qualities within the representations of objects, i.e. we have provided some local space and local time order for the objects of every real and possible experience. And if this is true *for every experience*, then the formation of intuitive concepts of space and time follows as a natural step.[35]

4.2   Theoretical Concepts of Space and Time

Intuitive concepts of space and time can take up an additional ontological burden, in order to play the role of either basic notions within philosophical views about nature (in "dogmatic" metaphysical teachings), or the role of theoretical concepts within physical theories that describe the kinematical and the dynamical aspects of moving bodies. Ready examples for this are the Newtonian and the Leibnizian concepts of space and time. While Newton supports a substantival view, Leibniz defends a relational view about space and time. Kant was well aware of the debate between S. Clarke (who defended the substantival view) and Leibniz. "There is no doubt that the debate between the Leibnizians and the Newtonians concerning the status of space and time forms part of the essential background to Kant's views throughout his career" (Janiak 2009, 2.1). There are interpreters who share the opinion, that accepting neither of these views, Kant developed his

---

[35]More details about the formation of the intuitive concepts of space and time can be found in 6.2, where an answer is provided to the question "How are the classical concepts of space and time possible?"

transcendental conception of space and time to surmount the weak points of the combating views.

I am not going to enter historical details here. We have seen all the same from the previous chapter that Kant, being rather a Leibnizian than a Newtonian at the time of writing his *Thoughts on the True Estimation of Living Forces*, completed in 1747, embraced the Newtonian view of absolute space in 1768 when his treatise "On the First Ground of the Distinction of Regions in Space" was published. It seems to me that this conceptual transition enabled Kant, though in a very specific sense, to make a resolute step towards his transcendental conception of space. The gist of Kant's argument of 1768 was that having in mind the existence of incongruent counterparts like left and right hands, absolute space does also exist and has a reality of its own.[36] No doubt, Kant defended then *an ontological conception of space*, and space was considered by him to be absolute and universal. Due to its universality space was accepted to be "not an object of an outer sensation, but a fundamental concept".

> Thus it is evident that instead of the determinations of space following from the positions of the parts of matter relatively to one another, these latter follow from the former... Since absolute space is not an object of an outer sensation, but a fundamental concept which first makes all such sensations possible, it further follows that whatsoever in the outline of a body exclusively concerns its reference to pure space, can be apprehended only through comparison with other bodies (Kant 1991, 32).

But if even a specific construction of a body that "exclusively concerns its reference to pure space, can be apprehended only through comparison with other bodies", then all outlines of bodies and their mutual relations become possible, just because of the absoluteness and the universality of space which encompasses all physical bodies and allows all the variety of their extensions. At that, space itself is not an object of outer sensation, but a fundamental entity that is a precondition for the possibility of all outer sensations. Such an understanding of space resembles its transcendental role as a pure and global sensuous intuition staying behind the synthesis of the matter of experience. As if Kant had to make one step to get into his later transcendental

---

[36]See the reconstruction of Kant's argument of 1768 in paragraph 2.2.

conception of space. But of course, this is only a speculative insinuation, because the "step" needed has proved to be a big conceptual leap.

Leaving this short speculative excursion aside, I would like further to show that being a Kantian does not preclude the possibility for a theorist to accept a corroborated contemporary conception about the spatio-temporal structure of the universe, and to accept for example the concept of *space-time* from Einstein's general theory of relativity. The latter concept is of the kind of concepts often bearing the name 'theoretical constructs'. They are abstract concepts of directly unobservable objects, which are basic constituents of the ontology of contemporary scientific theories. Terms like 'electron', 'quark', 'ten-dimensional string', and the like, represent theoretical constructs in the field of quantum theories. Space-time in the general theory of relativity is also a theoretical construct, or an abstract theoretical concept, because it refers to an imperceptible (as a whole, at least by humans) four-dimensional entity with variable curvature from place to place.

Even more, as we have already seen in paragraph 2.1, Stephen Palmquist argues that "Einstein's worldview had an essentially Kantian grounding" (Palmquist 2010, 53). In the second of a couple of papers then he shows how Kant's influence has guided A. Einstein for the rejection of absolute simultaneity and for his embracement of the relativity principle.

> Even though the physics of Kant's day did not present him with the empirical facts that prompted Einstein to propose his 1905 solution to the problem of simultaneity, Kant *did* recognize that in order to resolve the very different simultaneity paradox that did arise for Newtonian physics, one of Newton's basic assumptions had to be abandoned: space and time could no longer be regarded as absolute realities that exist apart from their relation to the human observer's mind (Palmquist 2011, 100).

If S. Palmquist is right, then the revision of classical physics leading to the birth of special and general relativity theories, accomplished by A. Einstein, would require a conceptualization of space and time in accordance with Kant's transcendental setting.

Now the problem which comes to the fore is how abstract theoretical concepts are acceptable from the point of view of Kant's philosophy. An answer to this problem will demonstrate that Kant's transcendental philosophy does not set up a conceptual barrier in front of the theoretical constructs successfully exploited by contemporary science, including the abstract concept of space-time.

Let me firstly remind that Kant himself accepted the correct usage of abstract concepts being already formed by the theoretical speculation of his day. Thus in the preface to the second edition of *Kritik der reinen Vernunft* (1787) he admits the reality of "the *invisible* force (the Newtonian attraction) which holds the universe together"[37], and speaks with confidence about the *invisible* magnetic matter (Kant 1966, 175, *CPR*, A: 226, B: 273). How do these abstract concepts have a legitimate use, if they have no directly observable referents in human experience?

Such kinds of concepts emerge as representations of *hypothetical* entities. However, Kant repeatedly brings out that "in the *mere concept* of a thing no sign of its existence can be discovered" (1966, 175, *CPR*, A: 225, B: 272). No matter how clear and complete a concept our faculty of imagination could produce, the concept *per se* gives no warrant for the existence of the referent of the concept. A scientist, however, can be highly convinced of its existence, and use the abstract concept in a legitimate manner, if the hypothetical entity, presented by its concept, agrees with the formal conditions of experience, from the one side, and is an essential part of the explanation of the observable features of the phenomena under research, on the other side. This is exactly the case with the concept of a magnetic field, or of "magnetic matter", as Kant once called it.

> A concept preceding experience implies its possibility only, while perception, which supplies the material of a concept, is the only characteristic of reality. It is possible, however, even before the perception of a thing, and therefore, in a certain sense, *a priori*, to know its existence, provided it hang together with some other perceptions, according to the principles of their empirical connection (analogies). For in that case the existence of a thing hangs together at least with our perceptions in a possible experience, and guided by our analogies we can, starting from our real experience, *arrive at some other thing* in the series of possible perceptions. *Thus we know the existence of some magnetic matter pervading all bodies from the perception of the attracted iron filings, though our organs are*

---

[37] (Kant 1966, XXXV-XXXVI, *CPR*, B: XXII, fn.), my italics

so constituted as to render an immediate perception of that matter impossible.[38]

It becomes clear now that Kant's transcendental idealism, valuing so high the productive faculty of imagination, does not raise any conceptual barrier in front of the intellectual production of theoretical constructs. Anyhow, they have to be produced in a very careful mode, since they have to satisfy certain requirements; and the Einsteinian construct of space-time makes no exception. Firstly, theoretical constructs must agree with the analogies of experience, or in broader terms (the properties of the non-classical quantum objects to be attracted as well), to follow a settled experiential pattern. Secondly, to account for the features of observable phenomena, just like the magnetic field accounts for the specific arrangements of iron filings. And thirdly, their introduction into a theoretical ontology must be guided by some well-articulated regulative idea, pretending to lend completeness to experience. Thus the idea that natural forces have a common source and origin has lead once to the successful unification of the electrostatic and of the magnetic fields into an electromagnetic field, and nowadays, to the unification of electromagnetic, weak, and strong interactions within a common theory, known as the Standard model of the quantum domain.

Abiding by the requirements just stated does not guarantee, by itself, the real existence of putative entities outside the limits of experience. Thus phlogiston, introduced in chemistry in the end of the 17th century to explain the process of burning, is expelled from contemporary science, in spite of the fact that it has practically satisfied the above requirements. Their *violation*, however, which allows the understanding to wander freely beyond the bounds of experience, can lead, most probably, through the dance of the fantasy, to the birth of imaginary or transcendent objects. Such objects, no matter how tempting our belief they might be, do not enlarge our knowledge. This is why Kant warns in the *Prolegomena*, that "the understanding begins its aberrations very innocently and modestly", to come in the end to the construction of a whole fictitious world. "This is the reason that young thinkers are so partial to metaphysics of the truly dogmatical kind, and often sacrifice to it their time and their talents, which might be otherwise better employed" (Kant 1997, Sect.35, 2.317).

But in spite of the fact that Kant is so stringent concerning the

---

[38](Kant 1966, 175, *CPR*, A: 225-226, B: 272-273), my italics.

usage of the understanding,[39] he is at the same time benevolent with respect to the faculty of imagination:

> The imagination may perhaps be forgiven for occasional vagaries, and for not keeping carefully within the limits of experience, since it gains life and vigor by such flights, and since it is always easier to moderate its boldness, than to stimulate its languor. (Kant 1997, Sect.35, 2.317)

And this is so, since deprived of "flights", imagination would not stimulate the production of theoretical knowledge, which is the core of the scientific enterprise.

REFERENCES

Janiak, Andrew. 2009. "Kant's Views on Space and Time". In *The Stanford Encyclopedia of Philosophy*, edited by Edward N. Zalta (September Edition).

Kant, Immanuel. 1883. *Kant's Prolegomena and Metaphysical Foundations of Natural Science.* Translated from the Original by Ernest Belfort Bax. London: George Bell and Sons, York Street, Covent Garden.

Kant, Immanuel. 1966. *Critique of Pure Reason.* Translated by F. Max Müller. Garden City, New York: Anchor Books.

Kant, Immanuel. 1991. "On the First Ground of the Distinction of Regions in Space." In *The Philosophy of Right and Left. Incongruent Counterparts and the Nature of Space*, edited by James Van Cleve and Robert E. Frederick, 27-33. Dordrecht / Boston / London: Kluwer Academic Publishers.

Kant, Immanuel. 1997. *Prolegomena to Any Future Metaphysics That Will Be Able to Come Forward as Science.* Translated by Paul Carus in 1902, and revised independently by W. Ellington in 1977 and James Fieser in 1997. http://web.mnstate.edu/gracyk/courses/phil%20306/kant_materials/prolegomena1.htm

Palmquist, Stephen. 2010. "The Kantian Grounding of Einstein's Worldview: (I) The Early Influence of Kant's System of Perspectives." *Polish Journal of Philosophy* Vol. 4, N 1: 45-64.

---

[39]"But the understanding which ought to *think* can never be forgiven for indulging in vagaries" (Kant 1997, Sect.35, 2.317).

Palmquist, Stephen. 2011. "The Kantian Grounding of Einstein's Worldview: (II) Simultaneity, Synthetic Apriority and the Mystical." *Polish Journal of Philosophy* Vol. 5, N 1: 97-116.

5 Does Big Bang Cosmology Resolve the First of Kant's Antinomies?

The problem does the world have a beginning in time, or not, falls into the content of the first of Kant's antinomies. Prominent cosmologists and physicists like Stephen Hawking, Paul Davies, and Steven Weinberg share the firm opinion that Big Bang cosmology presents a clear solution to this antinomy by pointing to the validity of the statement that the universe has a beginning in time. The aim of this chapter is to show that the antinomies of pure reason, the first one included, and the assessment of contemporary cosmology about the birth of the universe some 13, 72 billion years ago have different meaning and cognitive pretensions.

Key words: Kant's antinomies, Big Bang cosmology, beginning of the world in time.

As it was shown in paragraph (4.2), being a Kantian does not preclude the possibility for a theorist to accept a corroborated contemporary conception about the spatio-temporal structure of the universe.[40] It is no less interesting to shed light on the "opposite" point of view: what eminent contemporary physicists and cosmologists think about the first of Kant's antinomies of pure reason. It is well known that scientists subscribe today to the Big Bang cosmology accounting for the birth and the evolution of our universe. However, Kant had no (and naturally couldn't have any) idea about this contemporary cosmological theory, which does not support his first antinomy. The aim

---

[40]This contention follows from the validity of claim (C3), stating that Kant's transcendental philosophy does not set up a conceptual barrier in front of intuitive and theoretical concepts of space and time (see the *Introduction*).

of this chapter to this effect is to supply a negative answer to its title question, or in other words, to supply argumentation to claim (C_4). According to this claim, the conviction that the cosmology of the Big Bang grants a solution to the first of Kant's antinomies does not hold water (see the *Introduction*).

In the first paragraph of this chapter I shall adduce the firm opinion of eminent contemporary cosmologists and physicists like Stephen Hawking, Paul Davies, and Steven Weinberg regarding the first part of the first antinomy of pure reason, reducing my comments to a necessary minimum. In the second paragraph, on the contrary, the analyses of those opinions will prevail, against the background of Kant's intention concerning his first antinomy in particular, and the dialectical character of the antinomies in general.

5.1 Stephen Hawking and Others about the First of Kant's Antinomies

In his transcendental dialectics Kant considers four antinomies of pure reason, which represent the conflict of reason with itself, through the clash of transcendental ideas. The cosmological ideas comprising the first antinomy are stated as a thesis, and an antithesis.

Thesis: "The world has a beginning in time, and is limited also with regard to space" (Kant 1966, 306, *CPR*, A: 426, B: 454).

Antithesis: "The world has no beginning and no limits in space, but is infinite, in respect both to time and space" (Ibid, 307, *CPR*, A: 427, B: 455).

Both the thesis and the antithesis are supplied with their own proofs, and so an antinomy comes to the fore. The antinomy might appear to be an obstacle in front of human rational knowledge of the history of the universe. Stephen Hawking focuses primarily on the first part of this first antinomy of Kant's concerning a probable beginning of the universe in time, and contends that contemporary Big Bang cosmology, based on Albert Einstein's general theory of relativity, provides a resolution to it. In his bestseller *A Brief History of Time* he indulges in the following reasoning:

> The question of whether the universe had a beginning in time and whether it is limited in space were later extensively examined by the philosopher Immanuel Kant in his monumental (and very obscure) work, *Critique of Pure*

Reason, published in 1781. He called these questions antinomies (that is, contradictions) of pure reason because he
felt that there were equally compelling arguments for be-
lieving the thesis, that the universe had a beginning, and
the antithesis, that it had existed forever. His argument
for the thesis was that if the universe did not have a beginning, there would be an infinite period of time before any
event, which he considered absurd. The argument for the
antithesis was that if the universe had a beginning, there
would be an infinite period of time before it, so why should
the universe begin at any one particular time? In fact, his
cases for both the thesis and the antithesis are really the
same argument. They are both based on his unspoken assumption that time continues back forever, whether or not
the universe had existed forever. As we shall see, the concept of time has no meaning before the beginning of the
universe (Hawking 1988, 8-9).[41]

It is true of course that, according to the contemporary (and most
widespread) scientific picture of the birth and the subsequent development of the universe, "time has no meaning before the beginning
of the universe". Well, but as you see, Kant presupposes either an
infinite time through which the universe might had a real existence, or
an infinite time before it got started at a definite moment of time. So,
both the thesis and the antithesis, as Stephen Hawking insists, rest on
one and the same argument about an unlimited time, existing independently of the universe. But this "unspoken assumption" of Kant is
not correct, and thus his antinomy loses the conflict of the two cosmological claims. This tacit assumption of Kant is a relic from the strong
influence exerted on him by the Newtonian conception of absolute time
and space. This last assertion is not directly included in the adduced
quotation above, but as we shall see, S. Hawking explicitly supports
it elsewhere, and implicitly has it in mind here when saying that the
concept of time (in the Einsteinean universe of course) "has no meaning before the beginning of the universe". The Newtonian universe,

---

[41]The quotation goes on with the remark that time has no meaning before the
universe was created from a theological point of view, as well: "This was first
pointed out by St. Augustine. When asked: What did God do before he created
the universe? Augustine didn't reply: He was preparing Hell for people who asked
such questions. Instead, he said that time was a property of the universe that
God created, and that *time did not exist before the beginning of the universe*."
(Hawking 1988, 9), my italics.

on the contrary, inhabits an absolute space and exists in an absolute time that can afford itself to be an infinite entity, being independent of the universe. However, this has proved to be an obsolete and wrong cosmological picture, and thus, once again, Kant's first antinomy may be looked upon as resolved by contemporary science.

S. Hawking revisited Kant's "monumental (and very obscure) work, *Critique of Pure Reason*" once again in his lovely illustrated book *The Universe in a Nutshell*. He makes there a reconstruction of Kant's antinomy in the following way:

> Isaac Newton gave us the first mathematical model for time and space in 1687... Time itself was considered eternal, in the sense that it had existed, and would exist, forever. By contrast, most people thought the physical universe had been created more or less in its present state only a few thousand years ago. This worried philosophers such as the German thinker Immanuel Kant. If the universe had indeed been created, why had there been an infinite wait before the creation? On the other hand, if the universe had existed forever, why hadn't everything that was going to happen already happened, meaning that history was over? In particular, why hadn't the universe reached thermal equilibrium, with everything at the same temperature?
>
> Kant called this problem an "antinomy of pure reason," because it seemed to be a logical contradiction; it didn't have a resolution. *But it was a contradiction only within the context of the Newtonian mathematical model, in which time was an infinite line, independent of what was happening in the universe.* However, as we saw... in 1915 a completely new mathematical model was put forward by Einstein: the general theory of relativity. In the years since Einstein's paper, we have added a few ribbons and bows, but our model of time and space is still based on what Einstein proposed (Hawking 2001, 32-34).[42]

It becomes clear now, in accord with my previous comment, that S. Hawking refers the antinomical character of the considered cosmological ideas to "the context of the Newtonian mathematical model, in which time was an infinite line, independent of what was happening in

---

[42]My italics.

the universe". The Big bang cosmological model, based on Einstein's general theory of relativity, offers no room for the first part of the first antinomy of pure reason. The following clarification of S. Hawking is worth mentioning:

> The issue of the beginning of time is a bit like the issue of the edge of the world. When people thought the world was flat, one might have wondered whether the sea poured over its edge...
>
> In the early universe – when the universe was small enough to be governed by both general relativity and quantum theory – there were effectively four dimensions of space and none of time. That means that *when we speak of the "beginning" of the universe, we are skirting the subtle issue that as we look backward toward the very early universe, time as we know it does not exist!* We must accept that our usual ideas of space and time do not apply to the very early universe. That is beyond our experience, but not beyond our imagination, or our mathematics. If in the early universe all four dimensions behave like space, what happens to the beginning of time?
>
> The realization that time can behave like another direction of space means one can get rid of the problem of time having a beginning, in a similar way in which we got rid of the edge of the world (Hawking and Mlodinov 2010, 108-109).[43]

I'll go back again to this clarification in the next paragraph. For now two statements suffice as an "explanation" why Kant's first antinomy can be evaded in the context of the Big Bang cosmological model. The first one is that when we speak of the "beginning" of the universe, we must have in mind that "as we look backward toward the very early universe, time as we know it does not exist!" And the second statement is that if time behaves as another spatial dimension, then "one can get rid of the problem of time having a beginning, in a similar way in which we got rid of the edge of the world".

Paul Davies suggests a reconstruction of the first of Kant's antinomies, concerning an alleged beginning of the universe in time, in a manner quite similar to that launched by S. Hawking.[44] For this

---

[43] My italics.
[44] See (Davies 1995, 186).

reason I'll not quote it here. And because of the coinciding way of reasoning, Paul Davies suggests a resolution to the antinomy by the same theoretical argument of change of cosmological paradigms:

> Many people have an image of the epoch before the universe as a dark, inert, empty space. But for the modern cosmologist, neither time nor space existed before the big bang. The origin of the universe means the origin of space and time as well as matter and energy (Davies 1995, 186).

However, P. Davies realizes that this type of resolution of (the first part of) the first antinomy of Kant leads to another paradox. Let me call it "the paradox of the first event". This paradox and P. Davies' solution to it will be considered in the end of the next paragraph.

Steven Weinberg does not consider explicitly the first antinomy of Kant, but boldly criticizes his "intransigent metaphysics" that embarrasses the understanding that there are no moments of time before the Big Bang (Weinberg 1993, 137-138). To this effect he also does not see any antinomy in the clash of the cosmological ideas about the beginning of the world or its eternal existence. The theoretical ground of his firm opinion will be explicated as an example of a misunderstanding belonging mainly to the first type of criticism of Kant's transcendental conception of space and time, considered in paragraph (3.1). But this could hardly be assessed as a surprise, taking into account S. Weinberg's negative attitude towards philosophy in general.[45]

5.2 The First Antinomy of Pure Reason and Big Bang Cosmology

Does Big Bang cosmology resolve the first of Kant's antinomies? It seems that we can accept the positive answer. The contemporary Big Bang cosmology, based on the inflation model, successfully explains the birth and the successive evolution of the universe. And in so far as the age of the universe is estimated today to be about 13, 72 billion years[46], notwithstanding the impossibility this amazing period of time to be imagined by human consciousness, this period is a *finite* interval

---

[45]See the seventh chapter of his book (Weinberg 1993) entitled "Against Philosophy".

[46]This value of the age of the universe, based on precise observations, was recently broadly commented by Lawrence M. Krauss (2012).

of time. Thus the existence of the world has a beginning. But if so, we can say that the thesis in the first of Kant's antinomies is true, and the antithesis ought to be rejected. Contemporary scientific knowledge overcomes an antinomy, which appeared as a conceptual child of the classical Newtonian epoch of the growth of science.

Generally speaking, this is the conclusion that we can draw from the reconstruction of the antinomy suggested by Stephen Hawking, and also by Paul Davies, presented in the previous paragraph. It is my task here to analyze how pertinent is their solution to the first part of the first of Kant's antinomies. But let me firstly consider the adequacy of Steven Weinberg's position on the matter, since it conceals a way of thinking, common to the three eminent physicists, and probably to a great deal of contemporary scientists. According to S. Weinberg:

> Kant taught that space and time are not part of external reality but are rather preexisting structures in our minds that allow us to relate objects and events. To a Kantian the most shocking thing about Einstein's theories is that they demote space and time to the status of ordinary aspects of the physical universe, aspects that could be affected by motion (in special relativity) or gravitation (in general relativity)...
>
> This intransigent metaphysics comes to the surface especially in discussions of the origin of the universe. According to the standard big-bang theory the universe came into existence in a moment of infinite temperature and density some ten to fifteen billion years ago.[47] Again and again when I have given a talk about the big-bang theory someone in the audience during the question period has argued that the idea of a beginning is absurd; whatever moment we say saw the beginning of the big bang, there must have been a moment before that one. I have tried to explain that this is not necessarily so (Weinberg 1993, 137-138).

S. Weinberg's way of thinking, which ensures an easy exit out of the antinomy, conceals a mistake resembling the one of the curious listener to his lectures, who objects that there always must be a moment of time that precedes the moment of the Big Bang at which the

---

[47]With greater precision the age of the universe is estimated now to be 13, 72 billion years – see the previous footnote. S. Weinberg's book from which the present quotation is taken was published 19 years before Krauss' work (Krauss 2012).

universe was born. This way of thinking urges S. Weinberg not to have a bit of suspicion that there are natural entities called space and time, and because of this we should have only one notion of them, which more or less correctly represent those entities. Kant's notions are mistaken, while the corresponding notions of contemporary physics and cosmology are correct representations of space-time. But as we know, and has to keep it in mind, Kant's terms 'space' and 'time', and the corresponding terms in physical science, do not have one and the same referent. Space and time within Kant's transcendental conception are not concepts of physical science about whatever reality space and time might have as natural qualities or as constituents of the physical universe. As we know, they are pure forms of the human faculty for receptivity; they are pure sensuous intuitions, providing the possibility of any empirical intuition. To this effect they are void of any ontological meaning that is inherent in the theoretical constructs within physical knowledge representing the structure of the universe. Kant's transcendental 'space' and 'time' refer to human capacity for direct knowledge of the phenomenal world, and thus they bear a gnoseological burden, while 'space' and 'time' within physical theories refer to either natural attributes of the material world or to autonomous entities through which it exists, and thus they bear an ontological burden.

S. Weinberg seems to be aware of all this, having in mind the first sentence of his quotation. Yet he makes a methodological error *to compare Kant's and Einstein's notions of space and time, as if they have one and the same referent,* and to declare that "To a Kantian the most shocking thing about Einstein's theories is that they demote space and time to the status of ordinary aspects of the physical universe, aspects that could be affected by motion (in special relativity) or gravitation (in general relativity)." Let us recall now the similar declaration made by M. Čapek who tries to convince us that Kant "would be equally shocked by the Riemannian geometry as by Lemaître's and Gamow's cosmogonies assuming the finiteness of the cosmic past bounded by the initial 'zero-time'".[48] We already know both the root and the irrelevance of this shallow criticism of Kant. His critics shove their own realist understanding of space and time into Kant's transcendental conception, and then declare that Kant was wrong since a contradiction appears with the contemporary scientific picture of the universe.

---

[48]See fn. 30 in paragraph (3.2); (Čapek 1971, 43). The embarrassment with "the initial 'zero-time'" noticed by Paul Davies will be considered below.

It is no surprise that S. Weinberg sticks to realist concepts of space and time, having in mind his conviction that

> Physicists do of course carry around with them a working philosophy. For most of us, it is a rough-and-ready realism, a belief in the objective reality of the ingredients of our scientific theories. But this has been learned through the experience of scientific research and rarely from the teachings of philosophers (Weinberg 1993, 133).[49]

This kind of misunderstanding was analyzed in paragraph (3.1). Kant wouldn't be shocked neither by Einstein's theories that "demote" space and time depriving them of their previous Newtonian absoluteness,[50] nor by "Lemaître's and Gamow's cosmogonies assuming the finiteness of the cosmic past bounded by the initial 'zero-time'". Because space and time in Newton's classical mechanics, as well as space-time in Einstein's theories of relativity (special and general) are theoretical constructs of physical science, while space and time in Kant's transcendental philosophy have no such cognitive status.

S. Weinberg's way of thinking that brings about the considered misunderstanding is shared by S. Hawking and P. Davies, too. Even more, they look at Kant's transcendental conception of space and time as taken from, or as akin to, the Newton's classical cosmological model; because, as it is known, Kant was strongly influenced by Newton's mechanics. But classical mechanics rests on the theoretical picture of the absolute space and time, which on its part, was to be blamed for the birth of the first of Kant's antinomies.

Let me remind in this relation S. Hawking's statement from his *The Universe in a Nutshell*, that Kant's antinomy *"was a contradiction only within the context of the Newtonian mathematical model, in which time was an infinite line, independent of what was happening in the universe"*.[51] Further in this same book he declares:

> If the stars had just been sitting there forever, why did they suddenly light up a few billion years ago? What was

---

[49]S. Hawking would hardly say of himself that he is a "rough-and-ready realist", but this notwithstanding, as we shall see just now, he compares mathematical models of the physical world: the Newtonian and the Einsteinian one, referring Kant's conception of space and time to the Newtonian model of the universe.

[50]But that preserve the absolute character of space-time as a new theoretical concept in relation to the classical picture of the physical world.

[51]See fn. 42 from the previous paragraph.

the clock that told them it was time to shine? As we've seen, *this puzzled those philosophers, much like Immanuel Kant, who believed that the universe had existed forever.*"[52]

P. Davies is certain that "Kant accepted that to escape from his temporal dilemma would mean denying "the existence of an absolute time before the world," yet this he was not prepared to do" (Davies 1995, 186). Here once again the appearance of the first antinomy is explained by Kant's alleged acceptance of the model of the absolute time, taken from the theoretical basement of Newton's classical mechanics.

But how the depicted misunderstanding, attributed to the "critical" Kant, to Kant who considers the dialectical confrontation of reason with itself, becomes possible?

To my mind, there are three reasons for this. The first one is the already considered way of thinking, placing the transcendental notions of space and time on a par with the theoretical constructs of space and time, taken from fundamental theories of the physical world. The second reason is the popularity of the enduring criticism of Kant's transcendental conception of space and time (considered in chapter 3). As we have seen, some of Kant's critics, as M. Čapek and K. Popper, connect his conception of time and space with Newton's theoretical model of them.[53] And the third reason is that, as we know from paragraph (4.2), Kant's philosophy does not set up a conceptual barrier in front of theoretical concepts of space and time to be contrived by scientists as components of theoretical models, and dynamic models of the evolving universe included. To this effect Kant's transcendental conception of time could be easily, though incorrectly, dressed in the ontological garments, suited to the zeitgeist of the Newtonian intellectual epoch.

By imputing to Kant's transcendental philosophy a classical cosmological basement, eminent contemporary scientists like S. Hawking and P. Davies suggest a simple solution to the first antinomy of pure reason. As was pointed out at the end of the previous paragraph, it amounts to a change of cosmological paradigms:

> Many people have an image of the epoch before the universe as a dark, inert, empty space. But for the modern

---

[52](Hawking, 2001, 73), my italics. Here again S. Hawking binds Kant's conception to the ontological idea of absolute time.

[53]See paragraph (3.1), fn. 25. Let me remind also K. Popper's contention, quoted in paragraph (2.2), that "Kant... was convinced that Newton's theory was *true*" (Popper 1989, 190-191).

cosmologist, neither time nor space existed before the big bang. The origin of the universe means the origin of space and time as well as matter and energy (Davies 1995, 186).

If "for the modern cosmologist, neither time nor space existed before the big bang", then the world started its existence before some finite interval of time. So, the thesis that "The world has a beginning in time" within the first of Kant's antinomies comes out to be true, and the antithesis ought to be rejected.

This seeming conclusion, however, is based on *the above considered methodological misunderstanding.* The latter does not permit this conclusion to be accepted as a solution to the first antinomy of pure reason, despite that the claim that the universe has a beginning in time, taken as a separate claim, independent from the first antinomy of pure reason, is taken to be true by "the modern cosmologists". This claim has a different meaning in the context of Big Bang cosmology, while the first thesis of Kant's antinomy has another meaning in the context of the dialectics of the two confronting theses of pure reason. Within the antinomy they have a speculative origin and pretention that are different from the scientific meaning and pretention of the claim that the universe, as we know it from astronomical observations, started its existence 13, 72 billion years ago. S. Hawking "resolves" the antinomy, but under the false prerequisite that Kant embraces the ontological concept of time *"within the context of the Newtonian mathematical model, in which time was an infinite line, independent of what was happening in the universe".*[54] However, in Kant's transcendental conception and in the scientific model of Big Bang cosmology, time and space have different cognitive status.

Now I may say that the answer to the title question of the present chapter tends to the negative. But for a cogent argumentation of claim (C_4), central for this chapter, I must make an additional argumentative step. The first one, I've just finished, shows clearly that the declaration of some eminent contemporary cosmologists like S. Hawking, that the first antinomy of pure reason appears only because Kant was allegedly committed to Newton's theory of space and time, does not hold water. The second argumentative step I have to make is to show why Big Bang cosmology, with its highly corroborated claim that the universe has a beginning in time, does not resolve the first of Kant's antinomies, notwithstanding the fact whether Kant accepted Newton's cosmology, or not.

---

[54]See fn. 42 in the previous paragraph of this chapter.

I have already outlined the direction of this second argumentative step by the statement that within Kant's antinomy the first of its thesis (that "The world has a beginning in time") has another origin and meaning than the scientific claim about the beginning of the universe in the event of the Big Bang. I must explain further why this is so.

Kant's first antinomy must not be considered in separation from the other three antinomies of pure reason. All of them are explications of the four cosmological ideas of pure reason, according to the four categories (of the understanding) whose *absolute completeness* is being sought: of the composition of the given whole of all phenomena,[55] of the division of a given whole in phenomenal appearance, of the origination of a phenomenon in general, and of the dependence of the existence of the changeable in phenomenal appearance (Kant 1966, 300, *CPR*, A: 413, B: 440). As Kant firstly remarks, the idea of absolute completeness or totality refers to nothing else but the exhibition of phenomena and reason postulates the absolute completeness of the conditions of their possibility. Thus reason indulges in an absolutely complete synthesis, whereby phenomena could be exhibited according to the laws of the understanding.

> *Secondly*, it is in reality the unconditioned alone which reason is looking for in the synthesis of conditions, continued regressively and serially, as it were a completeness in the series of premises, which taken together require no further premises. This *unconditioned* is always contained in *the absolute totality of a series*, as represented in imagination. But this absolutely complete synthesis is again an idea only, for it is impossible to know before, whether such a synthesis be possible in phenomena... But the idea of that completeness is no doubt contained in reason, without reference to the possibility or impossibility of connecting with it adequate empirical concepts...
>
> This unconditioned may be either conceived as existing in the whole series only, in which all members without exception are conditioned and the whole of them only absolutely unconditioned – and in this case the *regressus* is called infinite – or the absolutely unconditioned is only a part of the series, the other members being subordinate to it, while it is itself conditioned by nothing else. In the former case the series is without limits *a parte priori* (without

---

[55]This idea underlies the first antinomy of pure reason.

a beginning), that is infinite; given however as a whole in which the *regressus* is never complete, and can therefore be called infinite potentially only. In the latter case there is something that stands first in the series, which, with reference to time past, is called the *beginning of the world* (Kant 1966, 301-302, *CPR*, A: 416-418, B: 444-446).

The four cosmological ideas, and the first one in particular that gives birth to the first antinomy, have their origin in the fact that human reason aspires to think the world not as *mundus phaenomenon*, where time is *a priory* form of sensibility attributing temporal order and permanence of the objects of experience, but as *mundus intelligibilis*, which leads to a deceptive reification of time. Such an illusionary substitution by pure reason is inevitable, because of the necessity of widening the conceptual applicability of empirical judgments about temporal and spatial order *among* phenomena, above the span of the faculties for receptivity and understanding, for searching of a beginning and spatial limits of the world as a whole, taken as a complete *totality* of phenomena. Thus the first cosmological idea gives birth to a thesis and an antithesis, as specifications of the two possible cases for construing the unconditioned, as pointed by Kant in the adduced quotation above. The *thesis* is based on grasping the unconditioned as an unconditioned "first" member in a series of conditioned phenomena, and states in this sense that *the world has a beginning in time*. The *antithesis*, on the contrary, is based on grasping the unconditioned "as existing in the whole series only, in which all members without exception are conditioned and the whole of them only absolutely unconditioned", and states that *the world has no beginning in time*. The antinomy is a result of the aspiration of reason to encompass the world as a whole, that is as a totality of phenomena. But this totality is not itself a phenomenon. It stays outside of the cognitive potential of the understanding, whose conceptual resource reason tries to make use of, out of the real or possible experience where this conceptual resource has only a proper usage.

Because of this pure reason could support both the thesis and the antithesis of a cosmological idea, and so the first antinomy appears in particular, which is a matter of interest here. Its thesis emerges as we have already seen, as one of the two possible modes of interpretation of the unconditioned in a series of consecutive phenomena. The thesis says of course that the world has a beginning in time. However, this statement is meaningful in the context of the antithetic of pure reason only, and is conceptually different from the scientific claim in the context of Big Bang cosmology, although formulated in the same words. The latter have here the status of *scientific concepts* with precise theoretical definitions: the world as the physical universe encompassing all (directly and indirectly) observable material and field structures and interactions, and time as a constituent of the universe as a fourth dimension of space-time.

As Kant further specifies, "the cosmological idea would always be either *too large* or *too small* for any *concept of the understanding*", independently of the way it realizes the unconditioned of the regressive synthesis of phenomena – whether in the manner of the thesis or in that of the antithesis.

> And this must really be the case with all cosmical concepts, which on that very account involve reason, so long as it remains attached to them, in inevitable antinomy. For suppose: –
> *First,* That the *world has no beginning,* and you will find that it is too large for your concept, which, as it consists in a successive regressus, can never reach the whole of past eternity. Or, suppose, *that the world has a beginning,* then it is again too small for the concept of your understanding engaged in the necessary empirical regressus. For as a beginning always presupposes a time preceding, it is not yet unconditioned; and the law of the empirical use of the understanding obliges you to look for a higher condition of time, so that, with reference to such a law, the world (as limited in time) is clearly too small (Kant 1966, 343, *CPR*, A: 486-487, B: 514-515).

The first antinomy of pure reason as an explication of the first cosmological idea emerges, because no real object of experience corresponds to the cosmological idea.[56] The thesis and the antithesis are by themselves sophistical (dialectical) propositions of pure reason, each one free from contradiction and thus giving rise to an antinomy.

> A dialectical proposition of pure reason must have this characteristic to distinguish it from all purely sophistical

---

[56]"It is possible experience alone that can impart reality to our concepts; without this, a concept is only an idea without truth, and without any reference to an object (Kant 1966, 344, *CPR*, A: 488, B: 516).

propositions, *first*, that it does not refer to a gratuitous question, but to one which human reason in its natural progress must necessarily encounter, and, *secondly*, that it, as well as its opposite, carries with itself not a merely artificial illusion, which when once seen through disappears, but a natural and inevitable illusion, which, even when it deceives us no longer, always remains, and though rendered harmless, cannot be annihilated (Ibid, 304, *CPR*, A: 421-422, B: 449-450).

So, the thesis and the antithesis of the first antinomy of pure reason are dialectical propositions which speculative reason must necessarily encounter in its ambition for obtaining a complete knowledge about a range of phenomena. But as dialectical propositions they are dogmatic and conceal in themselves "a natural and inevitable illusion, which, even when it deceives us no longer, always remains, and though rendered harmless, cannot be annihilated".

Principles and laws, as well as consequences of scientific theories and theoretical models are not dialectical propositions. And such is the claim that the universe came into existence before a definite period of time, which follows from Big Ban cosmology. Some scientific claims might prove to be false, contradictions may occur among claims of competing models, but such claims do not persist as equally provable thesis and antithesis of an antinomy, because of "a natural and inevitable illusion" of speculative reason. Sooner or later the scientific community will decide which out of two confronting claims to be accepted as an adequate one, and which to be dispatched in the realm of the history of science.

That the universe has no beginning in time is a classical scientific statement, which is revisable, and which was really revised. The statement that the universe has a beginning, in the context of Big Bang cosmology, is an opposite scientific statement that has been taken now to be true by modern cosmologists. On its part, the first thesis from the first of Kant's antinomies is a dialectical proposition of pure reason in its search for perfection of knowledge; it is a *persisting idea of reason that traces out some definite direction of human thought*. This dialectical proposition is an "inevitable illusion" that cannot be replaced by its antithesis (and vice versa) in the same way in which hypotheses are rejected on the basis of experiments and observations in the course of the growth of scientific knowledge. So, the conviction that the cosmology of the Big Bang supplies a solution to the first of

Kant's antinomies does not hold water. But this is just what claim (C_4) asserts.

Thus the argumentation in support of claim (C_4) has been completed, which was the chief aim of the present chapter.

Anyhow, some additional comments are needed here.

*

One may remain with the impression that Kant's transcendental philosophy does not pay due attention to the results of scientific knowledge, in so far as Kant's attention was attracted mainly by the antithetic of pure reason, thus leaving the epistemological role of fundamental scientific theories on the backstage of human knowledge. I will show that such an impression is not correct.

It is true of course that speculative reason has not a direct connection with experience, which is attributed to the union of the sensibility and the understanding.

> Reason never refers immediately to an object, but to the understanding only, and through it to its own empirical use. It does not *form*, therefore, concepts of objects, but *arranges* them only, and imparts to them that unity which they can have in their greatest possible extension (Kant 1966, 425, *CPR*, A: 643, B: 671).

This function of arrangement of concepts and of leading them to "their greatest possible extension" is accomplished by the ideas of pure reason. What is "the mechanism" of reason in imparting perfection to knowledge through concepts, borrowed otherwise from the understanding, being really a faculty for concepts?

We know that concepts can refer to their objects only through the schemata of sensibility. It is the schema that is both intelligible and sensuous, which allows the application of pure concepts of the understanding to the variety of phenomena. Well then, what can play the role of a schema, when concepts formed by the understanding have to produce some complete knowledge by the help of reason? Kant does not hesitate to say that *an analogue to the schema in this case is the idea of pure reason.*

> The understanding forms an object for reason in the same manner as sensibility for the understanding. It is the

proper business of reason to render the unity of all possible empirical acts of the understanding systematical, in the same manner as the understanding connects the manifold of phenomena by concepts, and brings it under empirical laws. The acts of the understanding, however, without the schemata of sensibility, are *undefined*, and in the same manner the *unity of reason* is in itself undefined with reference to the conditions under which, and the extent to which, the understanding may connect its concepts systematically. But although no schema of *intuition* can be discovered for the perfect systematical unity of all the concepts of the understanding, it is possible and necessary that there should be an *analogon* of such a schema, and this is the idea of the *maximum*, both of the division and of the combination of the knowledge of the understanding under one single principle... In this sense the idea of reason forms an analogon of the schema of sensibility, but with the difference, that the application of the concepts of the understanding to the schema of reason is not a knowledge of the object itself, as in the case of the application of the categories to sensuous schemata, but only a rule or principle for the systematical unity in the whole use of the understanding (Ibid, 436-437, *CPR*, A: 664-665, B: 692-693).

In a couple of words, the "mechanism" of imparting perfection to knowledge through concepts, borrowed otherwise from the understanding (being really a faculty for concepts) is realized through what Kant has dubbed "schema of reason". This is the general idea "of the *maximum*". I am not going to take up with terminological precisions here, but basic hypotheses, guiding the development of scientific knowledge, are just "rules or principles for the systematical unity in the whole use of the understanding", prompted by the application of concepts of the understanding to the schema of reason. So, *from one side*, objects are produced for the human knowledge *only* through the application of concepts of the understanding to the schemata of sensibility, and this is enough for the birth of (what is usually accepted to be) everyday knowledge. *On the other side*, concepts of the understanding could be also applied to the idea of pure reason, as a general schema of reason. This application does not provide "knowledge of the object itself, as in the case of the application of the categories to sensuous schemata, but only a rule or principle for the systematical unity in the whole use of the understanding". Thus theoretical hypotheses are being formed.

In this way Kant accounts for the origin of what is called today *ontology of a scientific theory*, in so far as such ontology is a systematical unity of hypothetical objects, governed by rules and principles, i.e. by laws determining their behavior. Hypothetical objects are represented by theoretical constructs. As was specified in paragraph (4.2), theoretical constructs "are abstract concepts of directly unobservable objects, which are basic constituents of the ontology of contemporary scientific theories. Terms like 'electron', 'quark', 'ten-dimensional string', and the like, represent theoretical constructs in the field of quantum theories." We have also seen that Kant's transcendental philosophy does not set up a conceptual barrier in front of the theoretical constructs successfully exploited by contemporary science, including the abstract concept of space-time. Kant hails the intellectual production of theoretical constructs through the faculty of imagination, provided they do conform to human experience.

> The objects of experience are therefore *never given by themselves*, but in our experience only, and do not exist outside it. That there may be inhabitants in the moon, though no man has ever seen them, must be admitted; but it means no more than that, in the possible progress of our experience, we may meet with them; for everything is real that hangs together with a perception, according to the laws of empirical progress (Ibid, 346, *CPR*, A: 493, B: 521).

Thus Kant accepts for example the reality of the magnetic field (called by him "magnetic matter"), notwithstanding the abstract character of its concept, since it "hangs together with a perception, according to the laws of empirical progress".[57] Moreover, *Kant values highly the role of mathematics in the formation of theoretical knowledge*, although he was not a witness of the accelerated development of theoretical knowledge in the natural sciences, being expressed by complex mathematical structures, since the end of the 19th century till present day.

> Even the true dignity and worth of *mathematics, that pride of human reason*, rest on this, that they teach reason how to understand nature in what is great and what

---

[57]See fn. 38 from the previous chapter.

is small in her, in her order and regularity, and likewise
in the admirable unity of her moving powers, far above
all expectations of a philosophy restricted to common experience, and thus encourage reason to extend its use far
beyond experience, nay, supply philosophy with the best
materials intended to support its investigations, so far as
their nature admits of it, by adequate intuitions.[58]

I hope the analysis carried out so far has managed to show that
Kant's transcendental philosophy really pays due attention to the results of scientific knowledge. My conviction to this effect is that proper
Kantians should not be (and probably are hardly) surprised by the
contemporary cosmology of the Big Bang.

*

In the end of the previous paragraph I mentioned that Paul Davies,
though not solving Kant' first antinomy, still gains a paradox that I
named *"the paradox of the first event"*. I'll try now to account for
the nature of this paradox. It is based on the usage of the classical
theoretical concept of time.

Some theoretical concepts refer to hypothetical unobservable entities, and some such concepts turn out to be fruits of erroneous hypotheses. They are rejected together with the falsification of the theory
from which they are a part. Such is for instance the fate of the concept
of phlogiston, taken from the chemistry of the 18th century. But not
only theoretical constructs of hypothetical unobservable entities may
bring sometimes problems for scientific knowledge. Problems may also
arise when common concepts of classical science are applied to a new
field of research. Such is the case with *the classical concept of time*,
taken as a theoretical concept from Newtonian mechanics. In the context of this theory time, to use S. Hawking's words, is "an infinite line,

---

[58](Kant 1966, 331, *CPR*, A: 464, B: 492), my italics. In P. Guyer's and A.
W. Wood's translation this same fragment is as follows: "Even the proper dignity
of mathematics (that pride of human reason) rests on the fact that since in the
great as well as the small, in its order and regularity, and in the admirable unity
of the forces moving nature, mathematics guides reason's insight into nature far
beyond every expectation of any philosophy built on common experience, it gives
occasion and encouragement even to the use of reason which extends beyond all
experience, just as it provides to the philosophy a concerned with nature the most
excellent materials for supporting its inquiries, as far as their character allows,
with appropriate intuitions" (Kant 1998, 496-497).

independent of what was happening in the universe".[59] This concept, however, ceases to be adequate in the context of the cosmology of the Big Bang. Within this theory time is neither "an infinite line", nor "independent of what was happening in the universe".

The inadequacy of the classical concept of time can be seen when one tries to answer a simple question, based both on the assumption that the universe (according to the Big Bang cosmology) has a beginning, and on the classical concept of time. The question is: "If the universe has a beginning in time, then which is the first event, connected with the first moment of its existence?" The answer to this question leads to the paradox of the first event.

> If time didn't always exist, then surely there must have been a discontinuity at which time abruptly "switched on"? And this means there would have been a first event – or First Event. The First Event can't be like other, ordinary events, because nothing came before it. It would be an event without a cause – a singular, supernatural event, surely? (Davies 1995, 186)

From the point of view of Big Bang cosmology the universe started from the so called singularity – a minute "egg", containing all the stuff of the universe. The idea of a singularity, from which the universe came into being through a Big Bang, is easily formed when one tries to imagine what happens with the constantly expanding universe, when looking from the present into the past. An imaginative excursion into the past of the universe would show a process opposite to that of an expanding universe. We shall expect a universe constantly decreasing in size when time is followed in a backward direction. This opposite process, as it seems, will come to an end into a singularity, thought to be a boundary state of the universe. In this state no space and time would exist anymore, because space-time had been stuck into a point with infinite curvature.

So, one can boldly say that the First Event we are looking for is just this singularity. But is this a plausible answer?

> Not exactly. There is a subtlety here. The singularity (which is in any case a mathematical artifact) is defined to be a *boundary* to time, not strictly part of time itself – not actually an event as such. The singularity bounds time in

---

the past, implying that time has not endured forever. Nevertheless, there need not have been a first moment (Ibid, 187).

And here the paradox emerges. If time has not endured forever, there must have been a first moment. And even if the singularity itself is not the First Event that is looked for, yet there must have been such an event, corresponding to the first moment of the existence of the universe. P. Davies' objection to this assumption is as follows:

> No. Is there a smallest number greater than zero? Clearly not. Try picking a number (one-billionth, one-trillionth...). That number can always be halved, and halved again, to obtain ever-smaller numbers. If time is continuous, then at no moment (one-billionth of a second, one trillionth of a second...) would there have been *no* preceding moments (Ibid).

It follows from here that there is no first moment of time in the history of the universe. But such a moment ought to exist, since the universe is not eternal and in this sense it has a beginning in time. So, we meet a paradoxical situation. Its origin is due to the involvement of the classical concept of time. This concept is built on the intuitive concept of time,[60] dressed in a mathematical garment, and thus rendered into a theoretical concept. This concept is the representation of time as a continuous line independent of the evolution of the universe. But in this case the beginning of time itself does not correspond to some first moment of it, which leads to the paradox of the first event.

There are two ways out of this paradox. The first one is to attract non-classical quantum effects that can provide a non-contradictory account for the beginning of the universe. This is P. Davies' solution.[61] The second way out of the paradox is an entire theoretical model of the history of the universe to be contrived, rejecting the classical concept of time as an inadequate one. This is S. Hawking's solution. He

---

[60]For the intuitive concept of time see paragraph (4.1).

[61]"It all changed, however, when physicists started taking quantum effects into account. The crucial property of quantum physics is that cause and effect aren't rigidly linked, as they are in classical, commonsense physics. There is indeterminism, which means some events "just occur" – spontaneously, so to speak – without a prior cause in the normal meaning of the word. Suddenly physicists became aware of a way for time to "switch itself on" – spontaneously – without being "made to do it"" (Davies 1995, 188).

has suggested such a cosmological model, introducing an "imaginary time" in it, which bears resemblance with the three spatial dimensions. Suggesting also his no boundary condition, S. Hawking succeeded in explaining the birth of the universe not out of a singularity, traditionally perceived as some mysterious initial edge of the universe.[62]

It is not my task here to consider the content of S. Hawking's solution. What was of interest to me was to show that although he does not resolve the first antinomy of pure reason (resolved on the base of the critical analysis of Kant himself) he succeeded in resolving the paradox of the first event.

REFERENCES

Čapek, Milič. 1971. *Bergson and Modern Physics. A Reinterpretation and Re-Evaluation.* Dordrecht: D. Reidel.

Davies, Paul. 1995. *About Time. Einstein's Unfinished Revolution.* Harmondsworth: Penguin Books.

Hawking, Stephen. 1988. *A Brief History of Time. From the Big Bang to Black Holes.* London. Toronto. Sydney. Auckland. Johannesburg: Bantam Books.

Hawking, Stephen. 2001. *The Universe in a Nutshell.* London. New York. Toronto. Sydney. Auckland: Bantam Books.

Hawking, Stephen and Leonard Mlodinov. 2010. *The Grand Design.* New York: Bantam Books.

Kant, Immanuel. 1966. *Critique of Pure Reason.* Translated by F. Max Müller. Garden City, New York: Anchor Books.

Kant, Immanuel. 1998. *Critique of Pure Reason.* Translated by Paul Guyer and Allen W. Wood. Cambridge: Cambridge University Press.

Krauss, Lawrence M. 2012. *A Universe from Nothing. Why There Is Something Rather Than Nothing.* Free Press. A Division of Simon & Schuster Inc.

Popper, Karl R. 1989. *Conjectures and Refutations. The Growth of Scientific Knowledge.* London: Routledge.

---

[62]For this kind of solution see (Hawking 1988, 143-149) and (Hawking 2010, 109-111).

Weinberg, Steven. 1993. *Dreams of a Final Theory. The Search for the Fundamental laws of Nature.* Vintage Books.

84

6

Paradoxes of Space and Time Conceptualized as Separate Entities and a Kantian Explanation of their Origin

Paradoxes of space and time, which appear as a result of their conceptualization as separate autonomous entities are firstly presented and analyzed. Such are some of the Zeno's paradoxes, those formulated by Sextus Empiricus and Aurelius Augustine, and recent paradoxes of the dynamic time. Then a Kantian explanation of their origin is put forward, and the problem about the flow of time, which provokes today a lot of philosophical controversy, is also considered.

Key words: dynamic conception of time, paradoxes of space and time, flow of time.

Even if not for space, we can hear sometimes the opinion that time simply does not have a real existence like that of the material objects. At that, both space and time are not perceived in the same way, as any one of these objects. According to the challenging words of Frank Arntzenius (2012, 125)

> We can see neither space nor time, we cannot smell them, we cannot touch them, we cannot hear them, and we cannot taste them. What, then, are these mysterious entities? *Why think they exist?*[63]

For one to take Arntzenius' question seriously and to say that space and time probably do not exist, would be the same thing as to deny

---

[63] My emphasis.

the reality of motion, because of the Zeno's paradoxes. We are so assured of the existence of motion, as well as of space and time, that if anybody would express some doubts about these things, she takes the risk to be looked upon as an eccentric, or even a crazy person. Yet, I shall try to show in paragraph (6.1) that paradigmatic solutions to the famous Zeno's paradoxes can be hardly admitted to fulfill their aim, and in (6.2) I'll direct a quick glance at paradoxes, formulated by prominent thinkers of late antiquity, like Sextus Empiricus and Aurelius Augustine, which still defy our common sense understanding of space and time. I mean the concepts of space and time as working notions of mundane and classical theoretical thinking, being taken to represent two separate autonomous entities.

But if the conceptualization of something leads to paradoxes, then this conceptualization ought to bear the brunt for the lack of cognitive success. There are two possible reasons for this. Either there really are some separately existing objective entities, to be called space and time, but our commonly accepted concepts of them represent inadequately those entities; or space and time are not entities with an autonomous existence, but nevertheless our cognitive faculty calls out clear representations of them just as separate entities, whose theoretical elaboration was crowned with the well-known concepts of absolute space and absolute time forged within Newton's classical mechanics.

Contemporary physics and cosmology, based on A. Einstein's theory of relativity, teach us that the universe we reside is characterized by one unique entity called space-time,[64] so space *and* time do not exist as separate autonomous entities. This fact then is brought into line with the second of the above mentioned alternatives: our cognitive faculty calls out clear representations of space and time, though the latter have no autonomous existence. It is not strange then that such "delusive" representations may lead our rational analysis into paradoxes, in spite of the conspicuousness and clarity of these representations. In paragraph (6.3) I'll try to account for the possibility of the presented paradoxes, including the hard problem why does time seem to pass, if there is no real flow of time. In so doing I'll provide argumentation to claim (C_5), which is the central claim of this last chapter. According

---

[64]In the classical relativistic picture of the world space-time is four-dimensional, while within the context of the so called M-theory, which encompasses the subject matter of the different types of string theories, space-time has eleven dimensions. The popular story of the very complex and yet unfinished M-theory, hypothetically admitted to be the expected theory of everything, can be found e.g. in (Hawking and Mlodinov 2010, 96-97).

to this claim transcendental aesthetic can provide a base for explaining the possibility of paradoxes stemming out of the conceptualization of space and time, taken to exist as separate autonomous entities (see the *Introduction*).

6.1 The Dynamic Conception of time and Zeno's Paradoxes

As I mentioned above, in (6.1-2) I'll present and analyze paradoxes that are typical for the conceptualization of space and time as separate autonomous entities. These paradoxes come from early and late antiquity, and still persist to defy human understanding, provided it tacitly accepts the validity of the so called *dynamic conception of time*. In a nutshell, this conception conforms to the men on the street's view about space and time. Reality is ascribed only to the present state of affairs in the world, which state of affairs corresponds to the present moment of time, or the moment "now". All past events are said to have no reality, since they do not already exist, and all future events have no reality either, since they do not exist yet. The material world possesses three spatial dimensions. Its history then is formally presented as a continuous evolution of *the* three-dimensional world through time.

Indeed, the dynamic conception of time has various theoretical specifications, known to epistemologists and philosophers of science as A-theories of time, to be opposed to the B-theories of time, accepting that time does not have a real passage. The vocabulary of a B-theory of time does not contain the A-terms 'past', 'present', and 'future', but is exploiting instead the terms 'earlier than', 'later than', and 'simultaneous with' for the events of interest.[65] I shall not enter this thematic field here, and I shall use occasionally the couple of expressions 'dynamic conception of time' and 'A-theory', as well as 'static conception of time' and 'B-theory' as synonymous.[66] What is of main interest to me here is the commonly accepted usage of the concepts of space and time that conforms to the dynamic conception of time. Space and time are accepted to exist as different aspects of reality, and every space or time interval can be divided into smaller intervals either

---

[65]For acquaintance with A- and B-theories of time see for instance (Dainton 2001) and (Mellor 1998).

[66]I'll not consider to this effect "intermediate" conceptions like that of the growing block for instance, which meet embarrassments of their own.

infinitely, or reaching a final limit, if space and time are thought to be discrete entities. It is just this widely accepted usage of the concepts of space and time that gives birth to the Zeno's paradoxes, as well as to those, pointed out by Sextus Empiricus and Aurelius Augustine.

Zeno's paradoxes are permanently attracting the philosophers' interest, resulting in hundreds of research works, as well as of popular essays in textbooks and websites. *They emerge in their quality of aporiae*, that is to say of impasses, of problem situations without an exit, what is the original meaning of the Greek word 'aporia'.

There is no unanimous opinion why Zeno formulated his paradoxes of motion. According to the standard and, as it seems, most popular view, he wanted to reject the belief that motion is a genuine process of spatial change through time, since its logical analyses lead to contradictions.[67]

There are two camps of thinkers. The shared opinion within the first camp is that Zeno's paradoxes have already obtained their solutions by using mathematical means or dialectical reasoning. Thinkers within the other camp reject this optimistic opinion. I'll try to show that they have strong arguments to do so.

Dichotomy

This paradox of Zeno has two versions. According to the first one a runner, starting her quick movement from point A, can never reach a final goal point B. The reason for this conviction is that the runner must firstly reach the middle of the way between A and B, then the middle point of the remaining half of the way, then the middle point of the remaining quarter of the distance to point B, and so on, and so forth. Since space is infinitely divisible, the runner has to pass through infinite number of points in a finite interval of time; and in so far as

---

[67]In one of the most philosophically profound dialogues of his – *Parmenides,* Plato gives the following explanation on the side of Zeno: "The truth is, that these writings of mine were meant to protect the arguments of Parmenides against those who make fun of him and seek to show the many ridiculous and contradictory results which they suppose to follow from the affirmation of the one. My answer is addressed to the partisans of the many, whose attack I return with interest by retorting upon them that their hypothesis of the being of many, if carried out, appears to be still more ridiculous than the hypothesis of the being of one. Zeal for my master led me to write the book in the days of my youth, but someone stole the copy; and therefore I had no choice whether it should be published or not; the motive, however, of writing, was not the ambition of an older man, but the pugnacity of a young one." Plato. *Parmenides,* 128c-e.

this is impossible, she will never reach the end point B.

The second version of "Dichotomy" states that the runner can never be set in motion, because before reaching the middle point between A and B, she must have passed through the middle point of the first half of the intended distance, but before that she must have reached the middle point of the first quarter of the distance, and so on. Thus there is no possibility for the runner to start her running process, which means that a movement from A to B is impossible.

Authors like Nicholas Fearn, for instance, see no difficulty in resolving the first version of "Dichotomy". In the times of Zeno, he contends, people had the false impression that a distance, composed of infinite parts, though diminishing in size, must be infinitely long. But it is known now that the sum S

$$S = 1/2 + 1/4 + \ldots + 1/2^n + \ldots$$

of the dichotomized segments of any distance included between two different points A and B is finite, and equals 1. Thus our runner covers a finite distance in a finite interval of time, and this is all.[68]

The first version of "Dichotomy" cannot be resolved, however, in the suggested way. What Zeno seems to have adduced as an aporetical argument is not the claim about the infinite magnitude of the sum S, notwithstanding whether he believed in that, or not. His argument is that the runner is not able to *actually* pass through an *infinite* number of spatial points in a *finite* interval of time. And exactly this impossibility implies the impossibility of motion, and hence, its non-reality.

The same reasoning is valid for the second version of "Dichotomy".

As it seems, the paradox could not be obviated by leaving its ontological background intact. Its central assumption is that space is a dense set of points, i.e. it is a continuum. A negation of this assumption is the claim that space is a discrete set of elements, or in other words, that its deep structure is a grain structure, that it is comprised of specific and further indivisible spatial atoms. To this effect there are authors who attract the ontology of quantum mechanics. But this step can hardly be of any help for seeking a plausible solution, since the quantum world exhibits complexities of its own. For example, we have no evidence, and we can have no evidence in principle, how a free quantum particle "moves" from point A to point B, and for all

---

[68]See the third essay "Zeno and the Tortoise" in (Fearn 2001).

90

we know, it could realize its "motion" in many different ways, each bearing its own probability for realization.

The ancient Aristotelian solution, making difference between actual and potential infinity, has certainly a heuristical merit (to be elaborated further by H. Bergson, as we shall see below), but offers no clear solution, too. This is the reason for Hegel to agree with Bayle's judgment that Aristotle's answer to "Dichotomy" is, uttered in French, "pitoyable".[69]

Achilles and the Tortoise

Let us imagine now that our hero is the legendary Achilles, who starts his quick run in a race with a slowly moving tortoise to be found 10 meters ahead of him. The curious conclusion in this paradox of Zeno is that the fleet-footed Achilles will never be able to overtake the tortoise in the running race – a fact that obviously contradicts our everyday experience. And it is just through this curious conclusion that the illusionary phenomenon of motion was meant to be proved once again. How this conclusion is made?

If we accept that our hero runs with a speed $v = 1$ m/s (one meter per second), and the tortoise moves ahead with a speed $u = 0.01$ m/s (one centimeter per second), after the first second from the beginning of the race Achilles is to be found one meter after the starting point, and 9.01 m behind the tortoise. After two seconds he shall be 8.02 m behind the tortoise, then 7.03 m behind it, etc. Although the distance between the two competitors is constantly diminishing, Achilles shall always be *behind* the tortoise, because during each interval of time in which he manages to reach the point where the tortoise was found in front of him, the slow animal will manage to pass a new distance ahead of him. Thus Achilles will never be able to catch up with the tortoise.

It is worth noticing that this paradox could be transformed into the first one, i.e. into "Dichotomy". If our coordinate system is not attached to the earth, but to the moving tortoise, then Achilles ought to cover the distance between his starting point and the immovable tortoise, a distance between two fixed points, A and B. This transformation is possible, because of the equivalent character of the two coordinate systems attached to two inertial frames of reference. This

[69]That is to say, piteous, deplorable (Hegel 1892, 269).

dodge provides no solution to "Achilles and the tortoise", however, unless we possessed a plausible solution to "Dichotomy", and this is not the case.

A "strides solution" is often put to the fore. In our case this suggestion for a solution takes into account that Achilles' stride per second is hundred times longer than that of the tortoise. So, ten seconds after the beginning of the race, Achilles shall be 10 m after his starting point, while the tortoise – 10, 1 m after it. After one more second the slow animal shall be 10, 11 m after Achilles' starting point, but Achilles himself – 11 m after it, which would mean that he has overtaken his competitor, and is already 0.89 m ahead of her. This commonsensical "solution", however, walks past the gist of the paradox, that in order to cover the 11 centimeters distance to the tortoise moving ahead of him, Achilles must accomplish infinite acts of crossing over the always remaining spatial intervals separating (the mass center of) his body from that of the moving tortoise for a finite interval of time, less than a second.

It could be also contended that the considered paradox has a mathematical solution, resembling the analogous "solution" to "Dichotomy". Let the initial distance between Achilles and the tortoise is indicated by d, the speed of the running Achilles by v, and that of the tortoise by u. The time needed for the swift-footed hero to reach the first position of the tortoise is $t_1 = d/v$. The time needed for him to reach the second position of the animal, which in the meantime has moved a distance ut_1, is $t_2 = ut_1/v$, the next third time for reaching the third position of the tortoise is $t_3 = ut_2/v = t_1u^2/v^2$, and so on, and so forth. Thus the time needed for Achilles to reach the n-th position of the tortoise is $t_n = (u/v)^{n-1}t_1$. The expression for the sum of the infinite row of time intervals for reaching the ever shifting ahead tortoise's positions is

$$T = \sum_{n=1}^{\infty} t_n = \sum_{n=1}^{\infty} (u/v)^{n-1}t_1.$$

This infinite row is a geometrical progression with a multiplier $u/v < 1$, and it is easily obtained that

$$T = d/(v - u).$$

This result means that our running hero can come up with his slow competitor in a finite interval of time that is as close to t_1, as v

is greater than u. This result completely agrees with everyday experience, but still can hardly be taken to be a solution of the paradox under consideration. And this is so, because, as it seems, Zeno's intention was not to deny that Achilles is able to catch up with the tortoise in a finite period of time, but that just within this finite period of time he can never actualize an infinite number of crossings of the spatial segments that separate him from the moving tortoise, no matter how a slow "runner" she is.

The Arrow

Probably, by this paradox Zeno wanted to show the contradictory nature of motion, not only when it is thought to be a process of transition through continuous space during the time flow of a finite time interval, but also when it is accepted to be a consecutive change of spatial places, which a moving body occupies in different fixed moments of time. By contrast with the former two cases, "The Arrow" is a paradox accepting motion to be realized not by virtue of the hypothesis about continuous time, but on the basis of the assumption that time is a sequence of discrete moments.[70]

Let us imagine the flight of a swift arrow, and let us also accept that time is a sequence of constantly changing indivisible moments, a permanent sequence of "nows" (of present moments). Within an arbitrary moment "now", the arrow has to be immovable, since if it were in motion, the fixed moment "now" should be divisible into parts, each corresponding to the places in space, occupied by the arrow. But this conclusion contradicts our premise that the moment "now" is further indivisible, being the smallest discrete interval of time. So, the time of the flight of the arrow is comprised just by such "nows", it is a sequence of discrete time intervals, and within every such "atom" of time the arrow occupies a fixed spatial volume, which is the place of the arrow corresponding to each specific "now". But it follows from here that the arrow is not flying at all, because *it is at rest within each "atom" of time*, and a sequence of states of rest can never produce a state of motion.

In order an exit from this aporia to be found, that saves motion

---

[70]Another argument of Zeno, known as *Stadium*, also leads to a paradox, if space and time are admitted to have a discrete structure, i.e., if they are constituted by "atoms" of space and of time that are not further divisible into smaller spatial or time intervals.

as a real phenomenon, some philosophers seek a refuge in dialectics. A dialectical solution to "The Arrow" is expected to be even universal to all paradoxes of motion as well, since this solution turns the paradoxical conclusions, traditionally taken to be a weak point in the philosophical defense of the reality of motion, into an argument in its favour. This transformation is based on evaluative change of the logical contradiction, from a negative into a positive feature explicated by the phenomenon of motion. And it was just "The Arrow" paradox that has given rise to the paradigmatic dialectical solution, or PDS for short, prompted by dialectical reasoning:

(PDS) In every instant the flying arrow *is* found, *and is not* found in a definite place.

The dialectical view accepts the truth of the phenomenon of motion together with its contradictory character. And if motion has to be treated in this way, it should be also claimed that it is *something more* than its standard trajectory presentation through a mathematical function of the spatial position of a moving body defined on the time variable. This is so, because the standard mathematical presentation of motion, being formal and thus a non-contradictory one, presupposes that a moving body has always a strict position in space corresponding to every instant from the duration of the process of motion. In this way, the standard mathematical presentation describes only *the effect of motion, but is not a presentation of its nature.* According to the dialectical treatment motion is *contradictory in itself.*

> In order to get movement into the picture, according to dialectic, we must recognize *both* that the body is at that place *and* that, in the same instant, it is also ceasing to be so. For our description needs to capture the fact not only that the body *is* where it is, but also that it is *moving* – hence in a process of change and becoming. For this contradiction is essential. As Hegel (. . .) says, 'something moves not because at one moment it is here and at another there, but because at one and the same moment it is here and not here.' (Sayers 1991, 87)

So, for a genuine (Hegelian and Marxist) dialectician motion (and more generally every change) is, in Hegel's words, an "existent contradiction", and this is the nature of motion, which in no way could be captured by pure mathematical or formal logical presentations. But can the dialectical approach, resulting in its paradigmatic claim that at every instant the flying arrow occupies and does not occupy a definite volume of space, be accepted as a resolution to Zeno's paradoxes?

I pose this question seriously, so I don't expect the probably correct, but trivial answer that dialecticians would reply with "yes", and non-dialecticians – with "no". What a philosopher cherishes above all in accepting a claim as a solution to a paradox is that claim to be grounded on a sound argumentation. This means that if behind the PDS stands a consistent argumentation produced in a proper dialectical pattern, then one must accept PDS as (at least a feasible) solution to Zeno's paradoxes, even if she is not an adherent to dialectics. But is this the case with PDS?

My answer tends to the nrgative. Although PDS rests on a dialectical formulation, it still lacks an appropriate dialectical argumentation. The notion of contradiction is central for dialectics. It results in the unity and the struggle of opposites. Moreover, the gist of the dialectical approach is the explanation of the dynamical phenomena in nature and the development of social processes through *solutions of the contradictions leading to some new state of affairs*. The latter is always an outcome from the struggle of the former opposites, and is expressed by a claim about *synthesis of a thesis and an anti-thesis*. But this well elaborated dialectical scheme is hardly applicable to the "Arrow paradox", i.e. to the paradox of mechanical motion. Within the phenomenon of mechanical motion the combating opposites are not clearly differentiated. The involvement of the abstract concepts of continuity and discontinuity for this purpose is still insufficient for a clear picture of opposites in a struggle, and the realization of a synthesis as a solution to the alleged contradiction is still more unclear.

PDS remains a very general statement, dependant on how the paradigmatic dialectical formula "A *and* non-A" is being interpreted, while there is no unanimously accepted interpretation among philosophers and logicians. Thus PDS can pretend for the most to be some conceptual framework for understanding the "Arrow paradox", but not a proper solution to it.

In his *Creative Evolution* Henry Bergson declares to have surmounted Zeno's paradoxes of motion.

> Take the flying arrow. At every moment, says Zeno, it is motionless... Yes, if we suppose that the arrow can ever be in a point of its course. Yes again, if the arrow, which is moving, ever coincides with a position, which is motionless.

But the arrow never is in any point of its course. The most
we can say is that it might be there, in this sense, that it
passes there and might stop there. It is true that if it did
stop there, it would be at rest there, and at this point it
is no longer movement that we should have to do with.
The truth is that if the arrow leaves the point A to fall
down at the point B, its movement AB is as simple, as
indecomposable, in so far as it is movement, as the tension
of the bow that shoots it... Suppose an elastic stretched
from A to B, could you divide its extension? The course
of the arrow is this very extension; it is equally simple and
equally undivided. It is a single and unique bound. You fix
a point C in the interval passed, and say that at a certain
moment the arrow was in C. If it had been there, it would
have been stopped there, and you would no longer have
had a flight from A to B, but two flights, one from A to
C and the other from C to B, with an interval of rest. A
single movement is entirely, by the hypothesis, a movement
between two stops; if there are intermediate stops, it is no
longer a single movement.[71]

The key point in this quotation is the bold claim that *"the ar-*
row never is in any point of its course". If this claim was not taken
seriously, then the other metaphorical contentions of H. Bergson to
the effect that the course of the arrow is an "extension" resembling
that of stretched elastic from point A to point B, and that the motion
of the arrow represents a simple and indivisible act, would sound no
more than curious assertions. Probably Bergson has learned well the
Aristotle's lesson that in considering Zeno's paradoxes one must give
up operating with actual infinity and thus must not direct her attention at the trajectory of a body that has already ceased its motion,
since the line of the trajectory is a dense and actually infinite set of
spatial points. The phenomenon of motion should not be explained
through its result, when a moving body has already stopped to move,
but should be construed as an "extension", as an indivisible bound
through space. So, the claim that an arrow starting from point A and
ending its flight at point B has passed through point C as well, has no
proper meaning, unless the arrow has stopped in C, is *motionless* in
C, and then has resumed its flight from C to B. Otherwise we cannot

---

[71]Bergson (1911, 308-309), my italics.

meaningfully assert for a body in motion that it is in point C at a definite moment of time.

H. Bergson pretends also that his conception about the phenomenon of motion provides a simple solution to "Achilles and the tortoise" paradox.

> When Achilles pursues the tortoise, each of his steps must be treated as indivisible, and so must each step of the tortoise. After a certain number of steps, Achilles will have overtaken the tortoise. There is nothing more simple (Bergson 1911, 311).

Can we accept Bergson's exhortation that "there is nothing more simple"? I think that the answer is "no", at least for two reasons. His suggested solution is but the already considered "strides solution" (see *Achilles and the Tortoise*), and we saw that it does not meet the conceptual challenge of the paradox. At that, his "simple" solution is not quite consistent with his own view of the nature of motion. Indeed, if Achilles has undertaken a swift run, then, as Bergson clearly insists, his body should be involved in an indivisible act of motion. But why then Achilles' steps should be considered separately from one another, as if the fleet-footed hero stops and resumes his dash with every step of him?

Let us turn back to the central idea of Bergson's conception of motion. It is expressed by the claim that a flying arrow is never found in any point of its course at any instant of the duration of its flight.

What does this claim mean, and what is its explanatory import for the solution of "The arrow" paradox?

At first glance, Bergson's central claim resembles the dialectical solution expressed by PDS. For in both attempts at solving the paradox it is asserted that at every instant the arrow does not occupy a definite place in space. We have come to the conclusion that PDS is not a proper solution to "The arrow" paradox, but mostly a conceptual framework for its construal. The case with Bergson's central claim is even worse, since Bergson does not even have the potential of the dialectical scheme at his disposal.

As for the explanatory import of Bergson's claim one may say that in its quality of a general assumption it could have the only pretension "to save the phenomenon" of motion, and not to explain its possibility and hence its reality. So, the proposed solution by Bergson to Zeno's paradoxes may remind us, on its part, of the old Bayle's qualification: "pitoyable" (see the end of *Dichotomy*).

6.2   Paradoxes of Sextus Empiricus and Aurelius Augustine

The paradoxes of Sextus Empiricus are *typical for the conceptualization of space and time as separate entities.* Being a sceptic he dares to argue that there are no such things as space and time.

Firstly, he considers *the concept of space* to be dependent on the concepts of place and of void in the "dogmatic" teaching of the Stoics. As Sextus writes:

> The Stoics call void that which can be occupied by an entity but is not so occupied, or an interval devoid by bodies, or an interval unoccupied by body; they call place an interval occupied by an entity and equal to that which occupies it (here calling bodies entities); and *space* an interval partly occupied by bodies and partly unoccupied (some say that *space* is the place of a large body, the difference between place and space being a matter of size).[72]

Then he analyzes the notion of place of a body and asks in what sense the place is "an interval occupied by a body". If the interval is taken to be only one (and I can add only two) dimension(s), usually called length, breadth and depth, then a place would not be equal to the object whose place it is; and so the very definition of place would be violated. If by "interval" all three dimensions are had in mind, then since in what is called a place there is found neither void, nor any other body having dimensions but only the body said to be in the place, and which is composed of its three dimensions, then "the body will itself be its own place, and the same thing will include and be included – which is absurd. Therefore there are no dimensions when a place is present, and for this reason there is no such thing as place" (Empiricus 2007, 177). This argument suffices for the conclusion that there is no such thing as space either, provided the second notion of

---

[72] *Outlines of Scepticism*, III, [124], (Empiricus 2007, 177), my italics.

space is taken, i.e. if space is meant to be simply a large place (see the end of the quotation above).

In order to reach the conclusion that space does not exist according to the first Stoic definition also, that is if space is taken to be "an interval partly occupied by bodies and partly unoccupied", Sextus suggests a dynamic consideration of place coming into being. The latter occurs when a body enters a void and its place is said to appear. What happens then with the void itself? It either remains or withdraws or is destroyed. But if it remains, then one and the same thing would be both full and void, which is absurd. If the void withdraws by some kind of motion, or is destroyed by changing, it would behave like a body. But it is absurd to say that a void is a body. Thus one cannot say that a void can be occupied by a body and become a place.

> For this reason, void too is found to be non-subsistent, since it is not possible for it to be occupied by a body and become a place, and yet it was said to be that which can be occupied by a body.
> *Space too is overturned at the same time.* If space is a large place, then it is overturned together with place; and if space is an interval partly occupied by a body and partly void, then it is rejected along with body and void.[73]

According to the Peripatetics, "a place is the limit of what includes insofar as it includes, so that my place is the surface of the air enclosing my body" (Empiricus 2007, 178). Sextus demonstrates, however, that this concept of place is contradictory,[74] as was the case with the Stoic notions of place. So, there is no such thing as place, and hence no such thing as space.

Secondly, Sextus considers *the concept of time*. As if anticipating the famous Augustine's confession[75] he acknowledges: "so far as the appearances go, there seems to be such a thing as time; but so far

---

[73] *Outlines of Scepticism*, III, [130], (Empiricus 2007, 178), my italics.

[74] This is so, because when a body is about to come into being at a certain place, this place ought to exist before the appearance of the body; otherwise the body cannot come into being in something that has no existence. But the place is affected by the surface of the body, which the place itself encloses, and for this reason it will not exist before the appearance of the body. It comes out that the place of a body exists and does not exist, which is absurd. Therefore a place is not the limit of what includes insofar as it includes. See *Ibid*, III, [131] (Empiricus 2007, 179).

[75] That he knows what time is when not asked, but he does not know when asked to explain.

as what is said about it goes, it appears non-subsistent" (Empiricus 2007, 180). At that, since time does not exist without motion, as some dogmatists contend,[76] then if motion is rejected,[77] time must also be rejected (Ibid, 181).

The ancient sceptic reveals five key paradoxes[78] inherent to the common notion of time being thought as a separate entity in the context of the dynamic conception of time.[79] Let me remind that this conception presents time as some flux that is immutably passing from the future to the present and from the present to the past. I'll adduce now only one of these paradoxes concerning *both the divisibility and the indivisibility of the present moment of time* for two reasons. First, this paradox suffices to shorn of the stubborn visibility that time is really flowing; and secondly, it is akin to a similar paradox explicated by St. Augustine to be considered below. *Here is the paradox ending with the conclusion that time does not exist*, because its three parts that compose it – past, present, and future times – do not exist:

> Time is said to be tripartite – one part being past, one present, one future. Of these, the past and the future do not exist; for if past and future times exist now, each of them will be present. Nor does the present. If present time exists, it is either indivisible or divisible. It is not indivisible; for things which change are said to change in the present, and nothing changes in a partless time – e. g. iron becoming soft, and the rest. So present time is not indivisible. Nor is it divisible. It could not be divided into presents; for because of the rapid flux of things in the universe present time is said to pass with inconceivable speed into past time. Nor into past and future; for then it will be unreal, one part of it no longer existing and the other not yet existing. (Hence the present cannot be an end of the past and a beginning of the future, since then it

---

[76] For instance, according to Aristotle's view time is "a measure of motion and rest".

[77] It seems Sextus has in mind here Zeno's final conclusion that motion has no real existence, though not explicitly referring to the aporiae of the famous Parmenidean disciple.

[78] If we leave aside the confronting "dogmatic" definitions of time, presented at the beginning of the section about time, since the very difference of theirs does not still lead us into a genuine paradox: one of the many definitions might prove to be relevant, at least in principle.

[79] See the beginning of (6.1).

will both exist and not exist – it will exist as present and
it will not exist since its parts do not exist.) Thus it is not
divisible either. But if the present is neither indivisible nor
divisible, it does not exist. *And if the present and the past
and the future do not exist, there is no such thing as time
– for what consists of unreal parts is unreal.*[80]

What a nice and well sustained argument for *the unreality of time*,
suggested 19 centuries before John Mc Taggart's attempt[81] aiming at
the same conclusion! But let us pay heed to the convincing logical
structure of Sextus' argument. Its conclusion is that time does not
exist, because past, present and future times do not exist, and they
certainly cover all that is meant by time. And if the parts which
compose the entire time do not exist, then time as a whole has no
existence either.

But can we, on the very ground of Sextus' argument, declare that
time does not exist; in spite of our experience that imposes its existence?

The answer to this question is by no means simple. One may reject
the rational structure of Sextus' argument, but as it seems this would
not be a reasonable act, since there are no sound arguments in favour
of such a rejection. What remains then? What remains is to agree
with the conclusion about the unreality of time, as represented within
the adduced argument. And this is exactly the common concept of
time as presented by the dynamic view of time.

In the eleventh chapter of his *Confessions* St. Augustine offers
a brilliant analysis of the dynamic concept of time attaining typical
conundrums concerning the explication of this concept. As was already
set out at the beginning of this paragraph, as well as within the context
of the Sextus' paradox, according to the dynamic conception of time
real existence is attributed only to the present events, to the world at
the moment "now", since past events no more exist, and future events
do not yet exist. And as is already known from Sextus' argument
against the reality of (the dynamic) time, the present moment reveals
a paradox: it is neither divisible, nor indivisible. A similar paradox
is offered by St. Augustine. He brought out that if the present time,
the moment "now", has any temporal parts, no matter how small they
could be in their temporal extension, these parts belong either to the

---

[80] *Outlines of Scepticism*, III, [144-146], (Empiricus 2007, 182), my italics.
[81] See (Mc Taggart 1908).

past, or to the future, and thus cannot constitute the present. How then we can estimate the temporal extension of the present?

> If any fraction of time be conceived that cannot now be divided even into the most minute momentary point, this alone is what we may call time present. But this flies so rapidly from future to past that it cannot be extended by any delay. For if it is extended, it is then divided into past and future. But the present has no extension whatever.[82]

If the present which is said to have a real existence has no extension, then the present would not exist, and if time is but a permanent change of present moments, then time would have no existence too. Hence we can conclude with certainty that the dynamic concept of time is contradictory, and to this effect has no objective referent. Yet we say that we experience shorter or longer time durations, inherent to different events like singing a song, finishing some kind of work, playing a game, and so forth.

The only option that remains then is dynamic time to be defined as mind-dependent. And this is exactly the step made by St. Augustine:

> From this it appears to me that time is nothing other than extendedness; but extendedness of what I do not know. This is a marvel to me. *The extendedness may be of the mind itself.*[83]

And also:

> *It is in you, O mind of mine, that I measure the periods of time.* Do not shout me down that it exists [objectively]; do not overwhelm yourself with the turbulent flood of your impressions. *In you, as I have said, I measure the periods of time.* I measure as time present the impression that things make on you as they pass by and what remains after they have passed by – *I do not measure the things themselves which have passed by and left their impression on you.* This is what I measure when I measure periods of time. Either, then, these are the periods of time or else I do not measure time at all.[84]

---

[82] *Confessions,* Book Eleven, XV, 20, (Augustine 1955, 184).

[83] *Confessions,* Book Eleven, XXVI, 33, (Augustine 1955, 190), my italics.

[84] *Confessions,* Book Eleven, XXVII, 36, (Augustine 1955, 191), my italics.

*

In the end of this paragraph let me summarize the conclusions we have reached about the concepts of space and time within the dynamic conception of time, and some suggestions to be further elaborated in the next paragraph (6.3).

Summary:

(1) The common concepts of space and time represent them to be separate entities, independent of one another, which are basic for the ontology of the dynamic conception of time.

(2) According to this classical conception the world exists in a three-dimensional space and constantly changes through time, which is composed of three separate (not overlapping) parts: past, present, and future.

(3) Zeno's paradoxes demonstrate the contradictory character of motion, which is traditionally accepted to take place in space and time, taken as separate entities, notwithstanding their continuous, or discrete nature.

(4) Analyses of space and time in the dynamic conception of time lead to paradoxes.

(5) If (3) and (4) are true, then the dynamic conception of time ought to be abandoned at least as a theory for the natural world, in spite of its observational backup. Its classical concepts of space and time as separate entities have no objective referents.

(6) It follows from (5) that we have to accept some version of the static conception, or B-theory of time.[85]

(7) If the theoretical step prompted by claim (6) is made, then one must have an explanation how the classical concepts of space and time are possible, why time is mind-dependent (see St. Augustine's conclusion), and why it appears to flow, if it does not really do so.

---

[85] About A- and B-theories of time see the beginning of paragraph (6.1).

(8) Kant's transcendental aesthetic can provide an explanation required by (7).

Claims (1) – (4) from this *Summary* have been considered in the previous and present paragraphs. Claims (5) – (8) are a subject matter of the next paragraph (6.3) of this last chapter. If their validity were presented in a convincing manner, then the general claim (C_5), which is central for this chapter, would be defended. It states that transcendental aesthetic can provide a base for explaining the possibility of paradoxes stemming out of the conceptualization of space and time as separate entities.

6.3 Kantian Explanation of the Origin of These Paradoxes

The *Summary* in the end of the previous paragraph consists of eight claims. The first four of them have already been defended. Our further task then is the consideration of items (5) – (8) of the *Summary*.

Claim (5) could hardly evoke any suspicion. It states that the dynamic conception of time ought to be abandoned, because its basic concepts, the classical concepts of space and time, lead to contradictions. But if a concept leads to a contradiction it can hardly be taken to represent some aspect of reality.

Long after the exposition of the key paradoxes of space and time related with the names of the ancient thinkers (that were considered in the previous paragraph), in 1908 John Mc Taggart showed that the common A-notion of time, or the dynamic concept of time, *is contradictory*. But insofar as only the A-theory of time can account for the genuine change of things in time, and since the A-theory is incorrect, there is no genuine change. Therefore time is unreal – a conclusion brought to the title of his famous paper "The Unreality of time" (Mc Taggart 1908).

Some philosophers do not take Mc Taggart's argument to be quite convincing, but I am not going to consider the strength of his argument here. The recent paper of Nicholas J. J. Smith suffices to be mentioned, in so far as he managed, elaborating Mc Taggart's argument, to demonstrate that the A-theory of time really leads to a contradiction (Smith 2011, 238-247). Paradoxes generated by the concept of dynamic time can be found also in (Prosser 2000, 495-496) and (Dainton 2001, 15-25). And once again it could be stated that because this concept of time leads to paradoxes and contradictions it must be rejected as a part of a consistent theory about space and time.

What has to be added, however, is that we may not agree with Mc Taggard's conclusion that if A-time is contradictory, then time at all should be taken to be unreal. We may turn to an alternative theory, which conceptualizes time in another way. It has to be a static conception of time or a B-theory of time – a step that is suggested by claim (6) in the *Summary*.

What such a static conception of time should look like? It would certainly be an advantage, provided this theory of time is a theory of space as well, and consistently unites space and time into a common ontological picture. A theoretic pretender for this role is Albert Einstein's theory of relativity. My arguments for this claim are the following.

First, A. Einstein's theory of relativity (both special and general) *exploits a static concept of time.* Time does not flow, but instead is a fourth world dimension; that is to say, time is geometrically interpreted.

Second, *the theory of relativity unites space and time into one and fundamental ontological concept of space-time.* This fundamental concept is not contradictory and does not lead to paradoxes, as was the case with the separate concepts of space and time within the dynamic conception of time.

Third, A. Einstein's special and general theories of relativity have been put to severe observational and experimental tests since their inception, and withstanding them, they have proved to be well corroborated.[86]

Fourth, a relationist view of space and time in the Leibnizean tradition, to the effect that only material particles and fields exist, which stand in certain *spatial and temporal relations*, meets conceptual difficulties, which are not met within A. Einstein's relativity theory in its quality of a "substantival" theory.[87]

The dynamic conception of time is based on the conviction, transferred also to Newton's classical mechanics, that if two physical events are simultaneous for one observer, they are simultaneous for any other observer as well. However, *the relativity of simultaneity* tells us that events which are simultaneous for one observer do not take place si-

---

[86]See in this connection Clifford M. Will (2005).

[87]A detailed argumentation of this claim is found in Frank Arntzenius (2012, ch. 5).

multaneously for another observer whose inertial reference system is in a relative motion with respect to the first one. A given event that will take place in a future moment (or has already taken place in a past moment) with respect to the first observer might be an event belonging to the present moment with respect to the second observer.

Let me give an example. Imagine that Mary is sitting at a table while she is accidentally pushing her glass of water over the edge of the table. Whether the glass *will be* broken or not when it reaches the floor after two seconds, is a *future* event for her. But it might be the case that for John, a second observer, being in a relative motion (with a great enough velocity) with respect to Mary, the non-broken glass, already lying on the floor, is an event belonging to the three dimensional space of his *present* events. Thus *one and the same event* – a glass on the floor with spilt water around it – belongs to a future moment for Mary *and* to the present moment for John.[88]

The considered event belongs to Mary's future. She does not know whether the glass will be broken, or not, when it will reach the floor, since the event (of the intact glass fallen on the floor) has not yet come into being *for her*. But *for John* this same event really exists, since it belongs to his present. We thus see that due to the relativity of simultaneity different events, being past or future events for some observers may also appear to be present events for other observers. None of the observers, however, has a privileged position in the four-dimensional world of the special theory of relativity; there is no "absolute", or privileged, three-dimensional space as a part of the four-dimensional *space-time* in the relativistic picture of the world. Past and future events for some observers are present, and to this effect existent events, for other observers. There is no absolute past, present, and future, these tense divisions are certainly meaningful, but only with respect to concrete observers. And since none of them is privileged with respect to the others, we come to the conclusion that *all events in the four-dimensional space-time have one and the same ontological status*, they are equally real. But if so, the four-dimensional space-time is actually given with all its events. This further means that it is a "static" world, a world that does not change, because *the time dimension is actually present as a constituent of this same world*, and it itself cannot undergo any changes, for the realization of which an additional

---

[88] For a lucid explanation why such things happen in the world of Minkowski, represented in the special theory of relativity by a four-dimensional pseudo-Euclidean space, see for example Roger Penrose (1989, ch.5).

(and global) time dimension would be needed. We thus see that the *actual presence* (one cannot say "existence", since this concept presupposes some time duration outside the time dimension within the four-dimensional world) *of the space-time* could be interpreted as a contemporary theoretical renovation of the ancient Parmenidean conception of one and unchangeable world. Within the contemporary philosophical jargon the conception is usually known under the name "block universe". It appears to be psychologically repelling name, and I shall not use it in what follows for this reason.

In so far as we have fulfilled the pretention of claim (6), we now come at the last two items of our *Summary* – the crucial questions in (7), which raise major difficulties in getting a plausible answer, together with claim (8). An explanation must be looked for how the classical concepts of space and time are possible, and then why time is said to be mind-dependent and clearly appears to flow, if it does not really do so. Let me start with the questions of item (7) in the order they are put in it, on the background of Kant's transcendental aesthetic.

So, how the classical concepts of space and time are possible?

A general answer is the statement that these concepts are being formed out of the direct human experience.

> There is no doubt whatever that all our cognition begins with experience; for how else should the cognitive faculty[89] be awakened into exercise if not through objects that stimulate our senses and in part themselves produce representations, in part bring the activity of our understanding into motion to compare these, to connect or separate them, and thus to work up the raw material of sensible impressions into a cognition of objects that is called experience? (Kant 1998, 136, *CPR*, B: 1)[90]

---

[89] In the original: Erkenntnisvermögen.

[90] The same excerpt from the "Introduction" to the second edition of the *Critique of Pure Reason* is translated by Max Müller as follows: "That all our knowledge begins with experience there can be no doubt. For how should the faculty of knowledge be called into activity, if not by objects which affect our senses, and which either produce representations by themselves, or rouse the activity of our understanding to compare, to connect, or to separate them; and thus to convert the raw material of our sensuous impressions into a knowledge of objects, which we call experience?" (Kant 1966, 2, *CPR*, B: 1). I prefer here Guyer and Wood's translation to be more adequate to the contemporary juxtaposition of "Erkenntnis" with "cognition", while "knowledge" is the English counterpart to "Wissen".

If all our cognition begins with experience, then the classical concepts of space and time, as concepts of separate entities, owe their formation to human experience. But Kant goes on with the important specification that:

> But although all our cognition commences with experience, yet it does not on that account all arise from experience. For it could well be that even our experiential cognition is a composite of that which we receive through impressions and that which our own cognitive faculty (merely prompted by sensible impressions) provides out of itself, which addition we cannot distinguish from that fundamental material until long practice has made us attentive to it and skilled in separating it out (Ibid, B: 1-2).

This important specification refers all the more to the common concepts of space and time. They really stay most close to experience, since no experience is ever possible out of space and time. Every empirical concept of any object is possible, because our cognitive faculty has space and time as *a priori* sensuous intuitions at its disposal. Well, but how concepts of putative entities called space and time *per se* are possible? To repeat Frank Arntzenius' words at the beginning of this chapter: "We can see neither space nor time, we cannot smell them, we cannot touch them, we cannot hear them, and we cannot taste them. What, then, are these mysterious entities? Why think they exist?"

Unlike any other empirical concept, the concepts of space and time are not formed "through impressions and that which our own cognitive faculty (merely prompted by sensible impressions) provides out of itself", because no hint of space and time is present into "the raw material of sensible impressions", but the experiential "material" itself is organized through the pure sensuous forms of space and time. Hence space and time are on the side of "that which our own cognitive faculty provides out of itself". This notwithstanding, we operate without problems with lucid notions of space and time both in our everyday life, and in the course of our classical physical theorizing. These are the classical concepts of space and time at the base of the already broadly commented dynamic conception of time.

Let me now go back to the content of chapter 4, dealing with the answer to the question how intuitive and theoretical concepts of space and time are compatible with Kant's transcendental philosophy. I am

not going, of course, to repeat what was already said there, but I need
to briefly remind the possibility for the very emergence of the classical
concepts of space and time.

My argumentation in paragraph (4.1) has started with the claim
that the pure *a priori* intuitions of space and time *are constitutive for
all objects of experience.* This being so, I have further noted that:

"Every object of experience appears as having a specific shape of
its own; two or more objects are spatially related, they are perceived
or imagined to coexist in some common part of space, and within some
common time interval. The transcendental ideality of space and time
provides the very possibility of every *empirical* intuition, and to this
effect, space and time are "empirically real". Shapes and durations,
spatial relations and time intervals could then be taken as belonging
to a general concept of space and to a general concept of time, these
concepts being formed as extrapolations out of experience: space and
time are notions of what still remains when substantive bodies are
driven away, or when a body is imagined to grow of volume or of
temporal duration to infinity. This transformative act gives birth to
space and time as utmost empirical concepts, by forming the belief
that extensions of objects and their outer relations, as well as their
successive temporal order do really exist, just because of the *existence*
of space and time."

But how this firsthand "ontologization" is possible? As we have
seen, Kant's brief and clear answer was this:

> The case is the same as with other pure representations
> *a priori* (for instance space and time), which we are only
> able to draw out as pure concepts from experience, because
> we have put them first into experience, nay, have rendered
> experience possible only by them (Kant 1966, 158, *CPR*,
> A: 196, B: 241).

The representations of space and time are formed as intuitive concepts, although not in the way in which usual concepts of empirical
objects are being formed through the very pure forms of sensibility –
space and time, but through a conceptualization of those forms ex-
tracting them back out of experience, since "we have put them first
into experience" and "have rendered experience possible only by them".
And as it seems for this reason, Kant himself adds sometimes the noun
'concept' to space and time:

We have already become acquainted with two totally distinct classes of concepts, which nevertheless agree in this, that they both refer *a priori* to objects, namely, *the concepts of space and time* as forms of sensibility, and the categories as concepts of the understanding (Kant 1966, 69, *CPR*, A: 85, B: 118).[91]

What is important for me here is that the formation of the concepts of space and time as pro-empirical (intuitive) concepts *is a very specific kind of concept formation*. While the formation of concepts "contains two very heterogeneous elements, namely a **matter** for cognition from the senses and a certain **form** for ordering it from the inner source of pure intuiting and thinking" (Kant 1998, 221, *CPR*, A: 86, B: 118),[92] in the intuitive concepts of space and time there is no one from the two above pointed heterogeneous elements. There is neither a matter of experience exploited by the senses, nor a "second order" pure super-sensuous form, to form the forms of sensibility.

Yet a **deduction** of the pure *a priori* concepts can never be achieved in this way; it does not lie down this path at all, for in regard to their future use, which should be entirely independent of experience, an entirely different birth certificate than that of an ancestry from experiences must be produced. I will therefore call this attempted physiological derivation, which cannot properly be called a deduction at all because it concerns a *quaestio facti*, the explanation of the **possession** of a pure cognition. It is therefore clear that only a transcendental and never an empirical deduction of them can be given, and that in regard to pure a priori concepts empirical deductions are nothing but idle attempts, which can occupy only those who have not grasped the entirely distinctive nature of these cognitions (Kant 1998, 221, *CPR*, A: 86-87, B: 119).

Having all this in mind we could say that the intuitive concepts of space and time are fruits of the human cognitive activity, which conceptualizes its own receptive capacities that allow, on their part, any

---

[91] My italics. The same excerpt is rendered by Guyer and Wood as follows: "Now we already have two sorts of concepts of an entirely different kind, which yet agree with each other in that they both relate to objects completely a priori, namely *the concepts of space and time*, as forms of sensibility, and the categories, as concepts of the understanding" (Kant 1998, 220, *CPR*, A: 85, B: 118), my italics.

[92] Original emphases.

object possession, in such a manner that space and time are transformed as separate concepts of specific entities. In fact, these pro-empirical concepts give an ontological birth to the classical concepts of the dynamic conception of time: the concept of a three dimensional space and one dimensional flowing time. The classical view of a three dimensional world of material objects that undergoes permanent changes in time has been easily obtained on the base of the classical concepts of space and time.

Thus I have made here an attempt at answering the question "How the classical concepts of space and time are possible?" which is the first question of item (7) in the *Summary*. This having in mind, the second question "Why time is mind-dependent?" has a relatively easy answer. Time is mind-dependent, because the classical concept of one dimensional time flux is firmly based on the intuitive concept of time, the origin of which, as we have already seen, is to be found in the "backward" conceptualization of the temporal order among objects of experience. This temporal order is secured on the base of the *a priori* pure intuition of time, or in broader terms, by the subject's mind. And this explains St. Augustine's frank avowal: "It is in you, O mind of mine, that I measure the periods of time."

This being the case, the question now comes to the fore: "Why the classical concepts of space and time conceal paradoxes, disclosed in paragraphs (6.1-2)?"

In the beginning of this chapter I conjectured that there are two possible reasons for this: "Either there really are some separately existing objective entities, to be called space and time, but our commonly accepted concepts of them represent inadequately those entities; or space and time are not entities with an autonomous existence, but nevertheless our cognitive faculty calls out clear representations of them just as separate entities, whose formal presentation was crowned with the well-known concepts forged within Newton's classical mechanics."

We have a good reason to choose the second horn of this dilemma. Space and time *are not* entities having an autonomous existence,[93] at least from the standpoint of the theory of relativity. Spatial and temporal intervals are certainly relative within the context of this theory, since they depend on the reference frame of an observer. What is not relative in the theory of relativity is the space-time being conceptualized as a four-dimensional reality.

---

[93]In this case entities whose measurable magnitudes are not different from the point of view of different observers.

Now an answer to the above stated question can easily be given. The classical concepts of space and time conceal paradoxes, because although they do not refer to entities having an autonomous existence, we operate with them, as if they do so. The material world is situated in a universal three dimensional space, and time flows in identical way for every observer. Our cognitive faculty is "to be blamed" for having just the *a priori* pure forms of space and time, which it really has, instead of some other united form to be adequate for the direct construction of four-dimensional objects at once. The answer which cannot be easily provided, however, is the answer to the question: "Why our cognitive faculty has just the *a priori* instruments that it has, and not intuitions of a kind, enabling direct representations of four dimensional objects?"

An attempt for a non-transcendentalist answer is being given by writers in the tradition of evolutionary epistemology. According to this tradition, the classical concepts of space and time have their epistemological roots in the firsthand empirical concepts of space and time, because the latter have provided good conditions for the survival of the human beings (from *homo erectus* to *homo sapiens*) in their natural, and further seemingly, in their social surrounding.

A transcendentalist answer would probably tend to explain that humans in their quality of limited knowing subjects could not principally possess pure sensuous forms for representing four dimensional objects at once. Because if they did so, then humans would be in a position to know immediately the entire history of arbitrary regions in the universe (i.e. to cognize the universe in its spatio-temporal integrity), which would mean having some kind of godlike intuition, being rather intellectual than sensuous. Humans are *temporal* creatures, because they do not possess any kind of intellectual intuition, but only sensuous intuitions, pure and empirical.

The good news is that the static concept of time in the theory of relativity *does not lead to paradoxes* analogous to the paradoxes concealed in the dynamic conception of time. But there is also a bad news concerning the static conception of time. This conception cannot provide, out of itself, an answer to the last question in item (7) of the *Summary*: "Why time appears to flow, if it does not really do so?"

This is an extremely difficult question to answer.[94] Of course, tran-

---

[94]"The notion that time passes is at once familiar and baffling. Everyone knows – or at least thinks they know – what it means to say that time passes. Yet when pressed for a description of the phenomenon it seems hard to avoid obscure

scendental aesthetic can provide a base for explaining this conundrum as well, as was the case with the already attained answer about the possibility of the key paradoxes emerging out of the conceptualization of space and time as separate entities. But an answer to the above question, based on transcendental aesthetic, could be only general and not quite informative. It amounts to the claim that time flows for the cognizing subject, merely because time as *a priory* form of sensibility is a *dynamic and diachronic mode of arrangement of events within human experience*. Thus the perception of a flowing time is a result of the "*a priory* essence" of this cognitive form of human sensibility. It is just its constitutive omnipresence for the formation of human empirical intuitions, which is responsible for the appearance of the Zeno's paradoxes. They stem out as a result of the classical ontological picture about the existence of space and time as separate entities that can be either continuous or discrete together, or separately. Each of these formal assumptions results in a paradox of motion to be viewed as a change of spatial positions through time. So, they appear in their form of *aporiae*, of paradoxical consequences without an exit. They have either no proper formal solution, or inspire dialectical speculations that seem to be promises for a solution offering no further detailed clarification (see 6.1).

By the answers to the three questions in item (7) the pretention of the last claim (8) in our *Summary* – that "Kant's transcendental aesthetic can provide an explanation required by (7)" – is fulfilled.

Thus far, I dare say that *enough argumentation has been supplied for the defense of the central claim (C₅) of this chapter*. As we well know, according to this claim transcendental aesthetic can provide a base for explaining the possibility of key paradoxes of the conceptualization of space and time as separate autonomous entities.

---

metaphors such as "passage," "flow" or "movement through time." Much has been written about other issues in the philosophy of time, but until the last few decades relatively few philosophers addressed the phenomenon of passage directly. Perhaps, like phenomenal consciousness in the philosophy of mind, it was considered so mysterious as to resist serious study by respectable philosophers; almost as though there were a whiff of the occult about it. But, as with consciousness, this has changed, and there has been a rapidly increasing interest in the notion of passage in recent years" (Prosser 2013, 315).

6.4 Additional Comments concerning Time Passage

As I pointed out, the last question in item (7) "Why time appears to flow, if it does not really do so?" is an extremely difficult question. Its appearance on the epistemological scene has become possible only after the birth of the new scientific knowledge borne by Einstein's theory of relativity with respect to classical Newtonian science. I would like to this effect to make some additional comments, *which are not directly connected with Kant's transcendental aesthetic.*

We have already seen that transcendental aesthetic can supply a *general answer* to the above difficult question. The problem whether a general answer is good or bad, i.e. satisfactory or unsatisfactory, is a matter of concrete theoretical interest. The answer I suggested was that time, as being *a priory* form of sensibility, is a dynamic and diachronic mode of arrangement of events within human experience, which urges human receptivity to reveal the world as a permanent succession of (un)expected events from the future becoming present, and of present events going into the past. One may also continue with the specification that it is just due to this pure *a priori* form of sensibility, that *the human mode of awareness* is but the consecutive grasping of three-dimensional space slices out of the four-dimensional world, corresponding to the "now" moments along the world line of every conscious observer. And it is exactly this perceptual splitting of the unified space-time continuum into space *and* time, or, in other words, it is *the way in which* the dimensional and the metrical qualities of space-time are being molded through the pure sensuous intuitions of *space* and *time*, which is responsible for the (dimensional and metrical) qualities of space and time *as they appear to us*, as if they are autonomously and separately existing entities.

This answer might be accepted as a good one by some philosophers, and even by theorists who have nothing in common with Kant's philosophy, but avow something as a "back door" for time in our minds. In the words of Paul Davies:

> There is no obvious "time organ" in our bodies in the same sense as we possess "sight organs" and "sound organs". Yet there *is* an inner sense of time – a back door – buried deep within human consciousness, intimately associated with our sense of personal identity and our unshak-

able conviction that the future is still "open", capable of being molded by our chosen actions (Davies 1995, 276-7).

The "inner sense of time", the metaphor about "a back door buried deep within human consciousness", imply that the time flux is a purely subjective way in which the – otherwise four dimensional – world is being perceived by humans. But is there in the representation of the flowing time, in the clear perception of change and duration, no objective aspect induced by reality? Is the concept of the *arrow of time* (for instance the time direction in which the Universe is constantly expanding, or the entropy is constantly increasing) not a lucid hint that the time flux *is not* merely of a subjective nature? Unfortunately, no concept of an arrow of time could be used as a solid proof that in our empirical intuitions of *things changing in time* there is something to be suspected as representing an *objective* feature of reality; in spite of the fact that the term 'arrow of time' can be accepted to name a fully legitimate concept.

> Many people muddle the flow of time with the arrow of time. This is understandable, given the metaphor. Arrows, after all, fly – as time is supposed to. But arrows are also employed as static pointers, such as a compass to indicate north, or a weather vane to show the direction of the wind. It is in the latter sense that arrows are used in connection with time... I discussed the fumbling attempts by physicists to pin down the arrow of time. The quality this arrow describes is not the *flux* of time, but the asymmetry or lopsidedness of the physical world *in* time, the distinction between past and future directions of time.
>
> Time does not have to *flow* from past to future for a time asymmetry to be manifested (Ibid, 256-7).[95]

Entering into the debate about the nature of the arrows of time would lead us astray from the matter of interest here. My aim was only to clearly bring out that *the phenomenon of the time flux has a subjective origin,* and this origin is "buried deep within human consciousness".

However, the transcendentalist approach to answering the tough question "Why time appears to flow, if it does not really do so?", as well as metaphorical expressions about some mysterious back door

---

[95]The emphases are original everywhere in the quotation.

within human consciousness (which are simply an awkward avowal for the feasibility of the transcendentalist approach), do not satisfy authors who suggest more informative theoretical models, based on the qualities of human memory, overlapping experiences, co-conscious pulses of experience, and so on, and so forth. I am not going to give comments to these well-known theoretical models, not because they are not interesting, but because each of them, besides some successful accounts for the emergence of the flowing time, manifests its own difficulties and flaws. None of them for this reason has been widely accepted as an established answer to our crucial question. These models are considered for example in Barry Dainton (2001, 93-109), and further analyzed by him in (2008, ch.3) and especially in (2013).[96]

> Even though it is one of the most familiar attributes of the physical world, time has a reputation for being deeply mysterious. Mystery is part of the very concept of time that we grow up with... Few people think that distance is mysterious, but everyone knows that time is. And all the mysteries of time stem from its basic, common-sense attribute, namely that the present moment, which we call 'now', is not fixed but moves continuously in the future direction. This motion is called the *flow* of time (Deutsch 1997, 258).

Indeed, "time has a reputation for being deeply mysterious" on the background of our knowledge that time does not really flow, in spite of our firm phenomenal awareness that time *does* flow. How can a B-theorist, e.g. a contemporary physicist accepting the theory of relativity, account for the mysterious time flux? It seems to me that a picture of "the work" of human consciousness to perceive changing objects and succession of events through time has been tacitly drawn for this purpose of late years. This picture could be dubbed *"the illuminating torch light of consciousness"*.

> Imagine waking up to find yourself in a strange place. You are sitting in a field of grass, next to a lamp that illumi-

---

[96] A recent attempt to account for the phenomenology of the flowing time was made by Simon Prosser who differentiated the phenomenal character of flowing time experience and its representational content. He developed "the hypothesis that the illusion of passage comes about because of the illusory and indeed contradictory way in which change is represented", although, as he noted, "I acknowledge that the view proposed here is far from the whole story about why time seems to pass" (Prosser 2012, 113).

nates the surrounding area. There is complete silence. As you look around, you can see nothing whatsoever. Apart from the small patch of grass illuminated by the lamp there is darkness everywhere. Not surprisingly, you conclude that you are alone. You could not be more wrong. A few yards to your right there is another lamp, and another person waking up to find themselves surrounded by total darkness; likewise to your left. In fact, you are in a line of people stretching for many miles in either direction, all of whom are sitting in their own small pools of light, all of whom are alarmed to find themselves alone in a strange place.

Why is it that nobody can see anyone else? The answer lies with the strange form of light emitted by the lamps, which only extends a few feet before dying away. *According to the B-theorist, we find ourselves in an analogous position in time. What stretches only a short distance is not light through space but consciousness over time: the temporal span of direct awareness is very brief. And as in the analogous spatial case, the fact that at any given time we are not aware of experiences occurring at other times does not mean that these experiences are not there.*[97]

Indeed, how the fact can be pictured that in any part of the conscious history of any individual person her past, present, and future experienced and going to be experienced events do have the same ontological status, but she is aware only of her present state of affairs, of the things she perceives just in the moment "now". All this prompts a picture of her consciousness as if illuminating only a very short span of her world-line going through the four dimensional space-time; as if her consciousness emits a narrow beam of awareness, a torch light directed onto the moment "now", and this beam of consciousness is permanently moving ahead and is illuminating one moment "now" after another. The rest of the segments of the world-line are existent, but not illuminated by consciousness, and correspond to either past or future experiences. A similar picture is exploited by David Deutsch to account for the advancing movement of the moment "now" along a straight line representing the one dimensional time (1997, 258-261).[98]

---

[97] (Dainton 2001, 29-30), my italics.

[98] In fact the illuminating torch light of consciousness moves ahead not along

Leaving this picture aside, the passage of time underlies every human sensation, awareness, internal and external experience. It is a profound feature of consciousness.[99] As Paul Davies (1990, 125) puts it:

> Our sensation of time is somehow more elementary than our sensation of say, spatial orientation or matter. It is an internal, rather than a bodily experience. Specifically, we feel the *passage* of time – a sensation which is so pronounced that it constitutes the most elementary aspect of our experience. It is a kinetic backdrop against which all our thoughts and activity are perceived.
> In their search for this mysterious time-flux many scientists have become deeply confused.

The omnipresent feeling of the flow of time, the "mysterious time-flux", is so deeply rooted in human consciousness that it seems to be

---

some unique time line, but as was already specified, along the four dimensional world-line (or better say world-tube) of every conscious observer, along which her proper time is measured. A more detailed analysis of this picture can be found in V. Petkov (2005, 148-152). The analysis is based on H. Weil's idea how the concept of time flow can be meaningful in a four dimensional world: "The objective world simply *is*, it does not *happen*. Only to the gaze of my consciousness , crawling upward along the life line of my body, does a certain section of this world come to life as a fleeting image in space which continuously changes in time" (Weil 1949, 116).

[99]In a recent paper Gal Yehezkel claims that "it is an illusion that we experience the passage of time, for such an experience is impossible" (Yehezkel 2013, 67). The argument for this claim is based on the premise that for every phenomenal experience which is contingent, if a person can experience something, she may as well have no experience about it. But since it is impossible to experience that time does not pass, it is also impossible to experience that time passes (Ibid, 70). There really is a problem here, but it is my contention that it is rooted not in this seemingly formal argument of Yehezkel, but in another argument of Simon Prosser that it is impossible to have an experience of time passing (2013, 321-325). Yet I say that *the passage of time is a profound feature of consciousness*, because 'the passage of time', notwithstanding the metaphorical charge of this expression, is intrinsically connected to phenomena like change, succession, and duration, calling up the sensation of time as flowing, which is concomitant to every human perception. "When we look through the window of a speeding train, we *see* the countryside flowing smoothly by. Holding one's hand under a running tap produces a tactile analogue: the flowing water is *felt*, and felt *as* flowing. If one listens to succession of (fairly brief) notes played on a piano, one is not only aware of each note as a temporally extended auditory occurrence, one also hears each note flowing into the next – the transitions between adjacent notes are themselves experienced" Dainton 2013, 389-390).

the very human way of revealing the world, nay, the way of being into the world for humans. These words are worth for a conclusion, yet I will add to them P. Davies' frank confession (1995, 278):

> Elucidating the mysterious flux would, more than anything else, help unravel the deepest of all scientific enigmas – the nature of the human self. Until we have a firm understanding of the flow of time, or incontrovertible evidence that it is indeed an illusion, then we will not know who we are, or what part we are playing in the great cosmic drama.

REFERENCES

Arntzenius, Frank. 2012. *Space, Time and Stuff.* Oxford, New York: Oxford University Press.

Augustine, Saint, Bishop of Hippo. 1955. *Confessions and Enchiridion, newly translated and edited by Albert C. Outler.* Philadelphia: Westminster Press.

Bergson, Henri. 1911. *Creative Evolution.* New York: Henry Holt and Company.

Dainton, Barry. 2001. *Time and Space.* Acumen Publishing Limited.

Dainton, Barry. 2008. *The Phenomenal Self.* New York: Oxford University Press.

Dainton, Barry. 2013. "The Perception of Time." In *A Companion to the Philosophy of Time*, edited by Heather Dyke and Adrian Bardon, 389-409. Wiley-Blackwell.

Davies, Paul. 1990. *God and the New Physics.* Harmondsworth: Penguin Books.

Davies, Paul. 1995. *About Time. Einstein's Unfinished Revolution.* Harmondsworth: Penguin Books.

Deutsch, David. 1997. *The Fabric of Reality.* Harmondsworth:Penguin Books.

Empiricus, Sextus. 2007 (seventh printing). *Outlines of Scepticism.* Cambridge University Press.

Fearn, Nicholas. 2001. *Zeno and the Tortoise. How to Think like a Philosopher.* New York: Grove Press.

Hawking, Stephen and Leonard Mlodinov. 2010. *The Grand Design.* New York: Bantam Books.

Hegel, Georg Wilhelm Friedrich. 1892. *Lectures on the History of Philosophy, Vol. I.* Translated from the German by E. S. Haldane. London: Kegan Paul, Trench, Trübner & Co., LTD.

Kant, Immanuel. 1966. *Critique of Pure Reason.* Translated by F. Max Müller. Garden City, New York: Anchor Books, Doubleday & Company, Inc.

Kant, Immanuel. 1998. *Critique of Pure Reason.* Translated by Paul Guyer and Allen W. Wood. Cambridge: Cambridge University Press.

Mc Taggart, John. 1908. "The Unreality of Time." *Mind* 17: 457-474.

Mellor, D. H. 1998. *Real Time II.* London and New York: Routledge.

Penrose, Roger. 1989. *The Emperor's New Mind.* Oxford University Press.

Petkov, Vesselin. 2005. *Relativity and the Nature of Spacetime.* Berlin, Heidelberg: Springer.

Prosser, Simon. 2000. "A New Problem for the A-Theory of Time." *The Philosophical Quarterly*, Vol. 50, N 201.

Prosser, Simon. 2012. "Why Does Time Seem to Pass?" *Philosophy and Phenomenological Research*, Vol. LXXXV, N 1: 92-116.

Prosser, Simon. 2013. "The Passage of Time." In *A Companion to the Philosophy of Time*, edited by Heather Dyke and Adrian Bardon, 315-327. Wiley-Blackwell.

Sayers, Sean. 1991. "Contradiction and Dialectic." *Science & Society* 55, N 1.

Smith, Nicholas J. J. 2011. "Inconsistency in the A-Theory." *Philosophical Studies* 156: 231-247.

Weil, Hermann. 1949. *Philosophy of Mathematics and Natural Science.* Princeton: Princeton University Press.

Will, Clifford M. 2005. "Was Einstein Right? Testing Relativity at the Centenary." In *100 Years of Relativity. Space-Time Structure: Einstein and Beyond*, edited by Abhay Ashtekar, 205-227. Singapore: World Scientific Publishing Co. Pte. Ltd.

Yehezkel, Gal. 2013. "The Illusion of the Experience of the Passage of Time." *Disputatio* 5, N 35: 67-80.

About the author

Anguel S. Stefanov is professor of philosophy in the Institute for the Study of Societies and Knowledge at the Bulgarian Academy of Sciences, and a corresponding member of the Academy. His main fields of research are epistemology and philosophy of science. Prof. A. Stefanov is head of the department "Ontology, Epistemology, Philosophy of Science" in the Institute. He has published 12 books and more than 160 papers containing original claims about the nature of space and time, as well as about the structure and growth of scientific knowledge.

www.ingramcontent.com/pod-product-compliance
Lightning Source LLC
Chambersburg PA
CBHW052114090426
42741CB00009B/1805